T0215398

Introducing Qt 6

Learn to Build Fun Apps & Games for Mobile & Desktop in C++

Ben Coepp

Apress®

Introducing Qt 6: Learn to Build Fun Apps & Games for Mobile & Desktop in C++

Ben Coepp
Köln, Germany

ISBN-13 (pbk): 978-1-4842-7489-7   ISBN-13 (electronic): 978-1-4842-7490-3
https://doi.org/10.1007/978-1-4842-7490-3

Copyright © 2022 by Ben Coepp

Managing Director, Apress Media LLC: Welmoed Spahr
Acquisitions Editor: Steve Anglin
Development Editor: Matthew Moodie
Coordinating Editor: Mark Powers
Copyeditor: Anne Sanow

Cover designed by eStudioCalamar

Cover image by Andrew Kliatskyi on Unsplash (www.unsplash.com)

Distributed to the book trade worldwide by Apress Media, LLC, 1 New York Plaza, New York, NY 10004, U.S.A. Phone 1-800-SPRINGER, fax (201) 348-4505, e-mail orders-ny@springer-sbm.com, or visit www. springeronline.com. Apress Media, LLC is a California LLC and the sole member (owner) is Springer Science + Business Media Finance Inc (SSBM Finance Inc). SSBM Finance Inc is a **Delaware** corporation.

For information on translations, please e-mail booktranslations@springernature.com; for reprint, paperback, or audio rights, please e-mail bookpermissions@springernature.com.

Apress titles may be purchased in bulk for academic, corporate, or promotional use. eBook versions and licenses are also available for most titles. For more information, reference our Print and eBook Bulk Sales web page at http://www.apress.com/bulk-sales.

Any source code or other supplementary material referenced by the author in this book is available to readers on GitHub (github.com). For more detailed information, please visit http://www.apress.com/source-code.

Printed on acid-free paper

Table of Contents

About the Author

Ben Coepp is a software developer, trainer, and author specializing in native C++ development as well as web development. He builds mostly web, mobile, and desktop applications. It is his hope that his work and writing can help you learn new things, experience the wonderful world of programming, and make you a better programmer or developer as well.

About the Technical Reviewer

Massimo Nardone has more than 25 years of experience in security, web/mobile development, cloud, and IT architecture. His true IT passions are security and Android. He has been programming and teaching how to program with Android, Perl, PHP, Java, VB, Python, C/C++, and MySQL for more than 20 years. He holds a master of science degree in computing science from the University of Salerno, Italy.

He has worked as a CISO, CSO, security executive, IoT executive, project manager, software engineer, research engineer, chief security architect, PCI/SCADA auditor, and senior lead IT security/ cloud/SCADA architect for many years. Technical skills include security, Android, cloud, Java, MySQL, Drupal, Cobol, Perl, web and mobile development, MongoDB, D3, Joomla, Couchbase, C/C++, WebGL, Python, Pro Rails, Django CMS, Jekyll, Scratch, and more.

He has worked as visiting lecturer and supervisor for exercises at the Networking Laboratory of the Helsinki University of Technology (Aalto University). He holds four international patents (PKI, SIP, SAML, and Proxy areas). He is currently working for Cognizant as head of cyber security and CISO to help both internally and externally with clients in areas of information and cyber security such as strategy, planning, processes, policies, procedures, governance, and awareness. In June 2017 he became a permanent member of the ISACA Finland Board.

Massimo has reviewed more than 45 IT books for different publishing companies and is the co-author of *Pro Spring Security, Securing Spring Framework 5 and Boot 2-based Java Applications* (Apress, 2019), *Beginning EJB in Java EE 8* (Apress, 2018), *Pro JPA 2 in Java EE 8* (Apress, 2018), and *Pro Android Games* (Apress, 2015).

Acknowledgments

This is my first book of this kind, and I am a little bit terrified by what people will think of me and my work when I release it to the public. But I hope it does well and that I can help others find their interest in Qt and perhaps learn something new.

I do want to thank my lovely girlfriend and future wife Bianca, as she listened to me rambling about this topic and the book for nearly half a year. I also want to thank my supporters on YouTube and the very friendly people online who asked me for a comprehensive guide to Qt for Qt 6. Most importantly, I want to thank the readers of this book. You are the reason this even exists, and I truly hope you found this interesting and that you learned something new. I am not as experienced as some other authors when it comes to writing books for teaching purposes, as my usual works tend to revolve around fantasy, so this is a big shift for me.

Special thanks to the great community that gave me the motivation for writing this book. Without the constant questions and problems people presented to me about Qt, I would have never written it.

I also need to thank Andy Shaw, who graciously read through parts of this book to find problems, and provided tips and tricks to polish it as much as possible. Without his help I do not think that this book would have turned out as it has. He helped me clear up a lot of the more unnecessary and problematic issues, and was instrumental in finding different things that I needed to do better.

CHAPTER 1

Introduction

Before getting to the content and tutorials for this book, this introduction will provide an overview of what we are going to do and how we are going to do it. If you would prefer to simply get started, you may refer to the Index or jump straight to **Chapter *2 Content***.

1.1 What Is This Book About?

I happen to like Qt and the development experience it offers. However, there is a lack of tutorials, videos, and books about it. You can learn it through experimentation and just trying out all the features, but that is less than ideal.

You could also go through the examples provided by Qt, but these are also not the best.[1] Providing a more organized, structured way of learning Qt was my motivation for writing this book, and by the end of it you should be able to make your own applications with Qt, whether they are mobile or desktop applications. This book does not claim to be the only voice on matters pertaining Qt, but it will show you how to best get started, which is the most important part.

What you'll see in this book is not the only way of using Qt or programming. In fact, the tutorials and examples I'll walk you through are probably different from what you'd find elsewhere. To achieve the things I want, I am willing to use any and all methods available. This simply means that I do not always use the "correct" method, but the one that best achieves the results I want.

---

[1] This does not mean that the examples are bad, but there are some parts that are out of date. They are still extremely great showcases, however, and can help you learn and understand specific topics in Qt.

B. Coepp, *Introducing Qt 6*, https://doi.org/10.1007/978-1-4842-7490-3_1

1.2 What Will We Be Doing in This Book?

This book will introduce you to several features Qt has to offer. You'll start by writing your first few applications while learning the concepts behind them. From there, you will learn more complex concepts and principles necessary to develop good applications. I will also cover most of the components that are relevant to making applications, at least those which you will use on a regular basis. And finally, you will create some programs with real-life applications.

What you would find in many available books are applications that might be considered good educational content, but not are not actual good applications. This book addresses that problem by bringing in my own work-related projects, which will best represent the type of work you will need to do. They are fun applications that I constructed in such a way as to make them as enjoyable as possible.

In general, this book is designed to teach you Qt and all the underlying concepts, principles, and elements, as well as general programming and development know-how. This will also be a major focus later in the book. The middle part of the book that reviews the components that Qt provides can also be used as documentation, and a place to look for specific solution or an example. The point is not to replace the Qt Docs; they may be outdated at some points but compared to a lot of other software documentation, they are extremely good.

By "outdated," I mean that if you are someone new learning Qt, you may notice that some parts of the documentation are better presented and more polished then others. This reflects the importance of the subject or component and how frequently it is updated and used. Specifically, I am referring to documentation such as the Qml Local Storage or QML Calendar that are still used and that new users might want to implement, even if they are not well supported anymore or are somewhat hard to understand. Chapter 3 of this book will be discuss this in depth, explaining some of the components that you will tend to use frequently through your development years but that might not be explained enough on the Qt Docs for a complete beginner.

Even if you are someone who is more experienced with Qt, you may nevertheless find some of this information useful.

1.3 Why Qt?

This is a question that you probably asked yourself before buying this book, or even before even starting to learn Qt. I'll explain here.

Qt is a cross-platform framework with which you can build applications on more or less every platform available, from your desktop or smartphone to even to your refrigerator. Qt runs on many devices. But what are the pros and cons of using Qt, and why are we going to use it?

Pros:

- **Qt easily works with multiple platforms.** Normally it requires a lot of effort or even multiple different frameworks to get your application onto multiple platforms, but Qt can take us a long way before we need to do anything else.

- **The amount of functionality.** This includes working with sensor data, touch control, and other great features, and there is also the entire power of C++ at our backhand. Therefore, you will be able to build everything with Qt.

Cons:

- **The steep learning curves.** Qt has a very steep learning curve, and it can be very hard for beginner to start working with Qt. That is the purpose of this book: to help you overcome the initial difficulties in getting started.

- **Sometimes Qt offers more then you need.** Qt has many features and elements that can do quite a lot, but there are not always necessary to achieve what you want. Therefore, it is possible to be overwhelmed with the number of options.

Despite these pros and cons, Qt is a wonderful framework with many uses, and there is a great community that is always growing and expanding. By contrast, many other frameworks (including hybrid and web apps) lack features. Some of them have a lot of functionality, but if you want to build something custom or not as common as other features, you are on your own and it becomes more difficult when the feature you want to build is more complicated. In my opinion this is not a very good option. Qt offers all that you need in very handy and easy-to-use packages that you can import when and if you need them.

1.4 What Are We Using?

As the title of this book suggests, we are going to mainly use Qt—specifically, Qt 6.0[2] and higher. This also comes with the Qt Creator and Qt Design Studio, which we are also going to use for all the application development we are going to do. If you already have some knowledge of how Qt works and you want to use your own desired IDE, then feel free to do so. But remember that all the screenshots as well as descriptions will be based on Qt Creator and Design Studio.

We also need Android Studio for the Android SDK, SDK Tools, and the NDK, all of which are essential for our Android development. I would also recommend getting something like Visual Studio Code or Atom as a Text Editor. While we are not going to use this here, because we can do everything we need to do in Qt Creator and Design Studio, down the line it would be helpful for creating specific files or writing code that is not highlighted as well as QML[2], such as JavaScript, which has little to no highlight at all. It is an option, however, so in this book I will mention it when it could be used. What will not be covered is the installation of Visual Studio Code or any other Text Editor or IDE, or assistance if something goes wrong while using them.

We will also be using the Qt SDK's, as is probably expected as we are developing Qt applications. We will go over how to install them later (they will be installed together with Qt Creator), and if you are wondering, the SDK is required to build Qt Application.

The development of applications for IOS devices will not be covered in this book.

If you want to know more about Qt or if you are interested in the Documentation of Qt, then please see `https://wiki.qt.io/Qt_for_Beginners`.

1.5 Signals, Warnings, and the Context

At times in this book I will want to add a bit more information beyond the basic instruction. This will be done in different ways:

- **Footnotes**

- **A different text color or *cursive* writing**

- **An image or screenshot, and accompanying description**

---

[2] For the projects we are doing it makes no difference which Qt version you use, as long as it is higher than 5.12.

These signals will only be used when there is a true need for them. Also remember to check out the page about the book on my website, where you will find additional passages as well as links to Git Hub, where I have a full repository with all the code and resources we use in the project. These resources are not needed for the instruction covered in this book, but are available to you if you have questions that are not answered in the book or are not as clear as you want them to be.

The content and the information I want to teach is the most important part of this book. You will see that I tend to use screenshots on a very regular basis; all screenshots were created using Qt 6 as it is the current version, but if you are running any current version of Qt then all screenshots still hold true. Sometimes I will also use code snippets if I want to show you a lot of code at once.

CHAPTER 2

Content

It is recommended that you read the content in this book in order so as not to lose focus or miss something important. Later on you may want to jump straight to a specific topic or subject that interests you, which you can do by referring to the index.

2.1 Setting Up the Tools

Before using Qt, we must download and install all of the necessary tools, software, SDKs, and NDKs.[1] I highly recommend that you install anything you are missing. With the exception of Android Studio and Qt, as well as Qt Creator, you can use whatever tool, IDE, or text editor you prefer. Please remember that if you choose your own tools you might encounter problems or warnings beyond the scope of this book.[2]

2.1.1 Downloading + Installing Qt

The first step is to get Qt, and the best way to do this is through their website (`https://www.qt.io/`).

---

[1]SDKs and NDKs are fundamental in any development project, because they include all the files and data you need to develop your applications.

[2]When you stumble across problems like this you can always send me an email or leave a question on the Amazon page for this book, and I will try to help you.

© Ben Coepp 2022
B. Coepp, *Introducing Qt 6*, https://doi.org/10.1007/978-1-4842-7490-3_2

www.qt.io ▾ Diese Seite übersetzen

Qt | Cross-platform software development for embedded ...

Qt is the faster, smarter way to create innovative devices, modern UIs & applications for multiple screens. Cross-platform software development at its best.

Du hast diese Seite 4 Mal aufgerufen. Letzter Besuch: 01.11.20

Download
With Qt, you can reach all your target platforms – desktop ...

Developers
1 million software developers love Qt because they can build ...

Qt Creator IDE
Qt is a cross-platform framework with multiple tools. Qt supports ...

Qt Documentation
Qt 5.15 - Python - C++ - Getting Started with Qt - Qt Wiki - Qt 5.9

Open Source
The Qt framework is available under both open source and ...

Features
Explore the features of the latest Qt version to see Qt features and ...

Google Search of Qt

The homepage of Qt provides information about the product and the services the Qt Company provides. For downloading and installing, the important part is at the top of the screen.

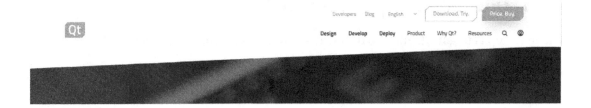

Qt Website Top-Bar

Clicking the *Download. Try.* button will bring us to the next part. If you want to buy Qt, then you can also click the green *Buy Now.* button, but for our needs this is not necessary; Qt has a good Open-Source base that has all the features needed for most developers, and I never needed anything else while using Qt. There are only a few features that can be bought with the commercial license, and you only need it if you want to make money selling and providing an application.

Next, scroll down to the different download links and click on the green button that says *Go open source*. This will take you to the next section.

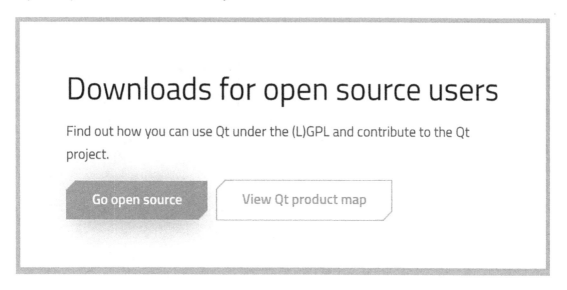

Download Card for Open-Source Users

Here you also need to scroll down near the bottom of the page and click on *Download the Qt Online Installer*. This will bring you to the final page we need to visit on their website:

Here you only need to click on the *Download* button, which will download the installer.

Your download

We detected your operating system as: Windows
Recommended download: Qt Online Installer for Windows

Not the installer you need? View other options.

The installer will ask you to sign in using your Qt account credentials. This
will ensure you get the right access to the right components, such as those
under a commercial license.

Please note:

If you requested a 30-day commercial trial extension or an additional license
for embedded components, we will contact you shortly. In the meantime,
please get started with Qt.

If you are installing under a **Qt open source license**, please **be sure you are
in full compliance** with the legal obligations of the (L)GPL v2/3 **before
installation**. For a brief overview visit the main download page or for more
details see the FAQ.

At this point you can close the browser and start the installer.

The installation will take a while, but meanwhile, just follow the prompts in the
following screenshots:

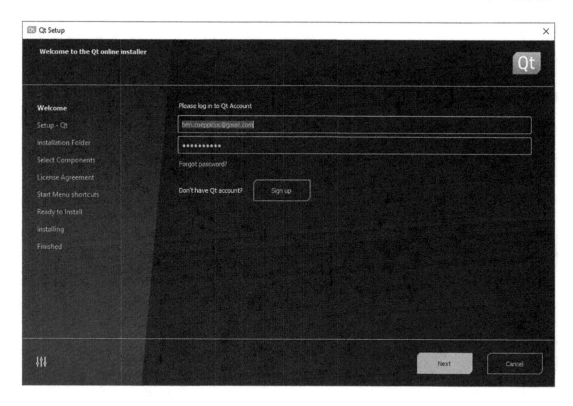

Login Form of the Qt Installer

Here you need to just put in your Qt account name and password. If you do not already have an account, then you can click the Sign-Up link and create an account. Creating an account is mandatory.

If you already have an account, then you fill out the two input forms and then click next.

Qt open source runs under the GNU General Public License v3.[3] Therefore, you cannot use this version of Qt we downloaded, as the installer for it is for commercial use.

---

[3] The GNU General Public License v3 is a special License that allows you to use Qt and its Components and Features for noncommercial use, available at https://www.qt.io/licensing/.

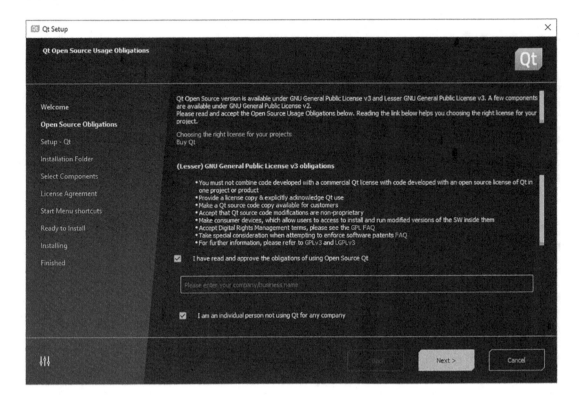

Qt License Agreement

Next, you need to check that you have read and approved of the license agreements by either typing in your company's name or checking the box by "I am an individual." If you have done both, then Next will be enabled and we can continue.[4]

The following page can be ignored. For our purposes we do not need a commercial license, so click Next and continue.

---

[4] Qt is not that large of a company compared to other companies like Amazon or Microsoft. If you want to make money selling an app or providing some other kind of monetary service, please buy a Qt license. It helps the company finance the development, and you will not have legal problems.

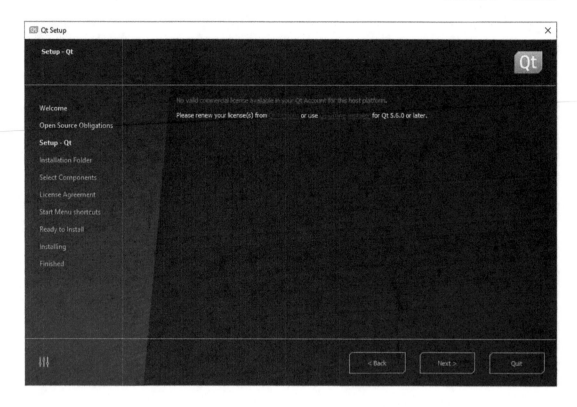

Expired License Page, you can ignore this here

The installer will now retrieve some metainformation and then download it. Depending on your Internet connection, this can take a while.

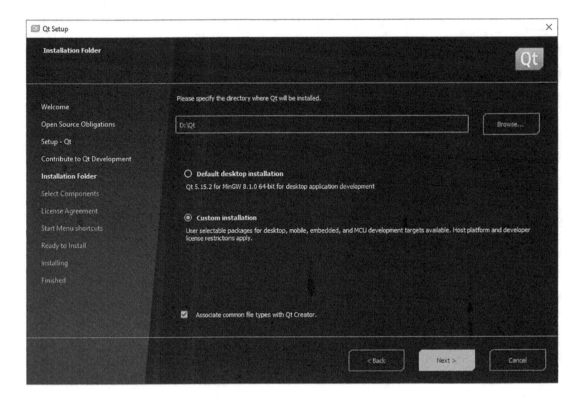

Location Page as well as installation type

Next, the installer asks if you want to provide usage data, crash reports, and general statistics to the Qt Company. I prefer to check the first box and let them use my data, but this choice is up to you. After you select your choice, click Next.

If wish to change this preference later, then you can launch the Qt Maintenance Tool, where you can adjust this setting.

On the next page the installer asks you to select the installation path, and to indicate whether you want a custom installation or the default desktop installation. Here we will leave everything as it is and click next. If you wish, you can chose your own installation folder and even select the default desktop installation. Just do not check the box in the bottom left. Now, click Next.

This is the most important step in the installer and the one that can have a negative impact on your development environment. We will not be using a preview version of Qt, but instead a stable release. For this, you need to click on the Qt drop-down and expand it.

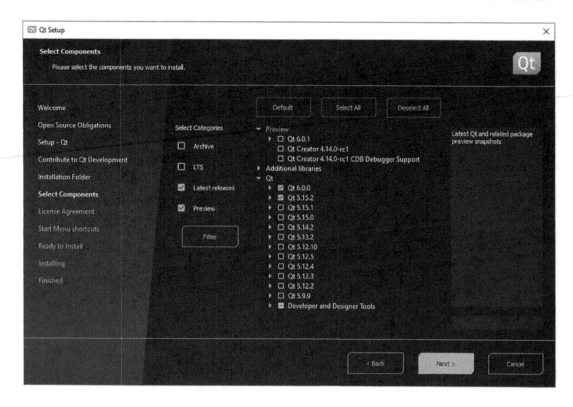

Here you can choose the kits and tools

This will pop open a drop-down with many different Qt versions. We want the newest version, so check Qt 6 and open the Qt 6 drop-down.

Here you can find many different packages that Qt ships with a normal installation. For a beginner, I recommend just leaving everything as it is and continuing. Note that Qt takes up a lot of space (above 50 GB), so if you do not have that much space on your hard drive then you might want to remove some of the libraries or packages. Things we will not need are Web Assembly, MSVC, and UWP. Everything else is needed and should be included.

It is worth having all the available resources as well as tools and features right from the beginning, as they can help you start out immediately with a new project. You do not need to search for the right tool; you can just start.

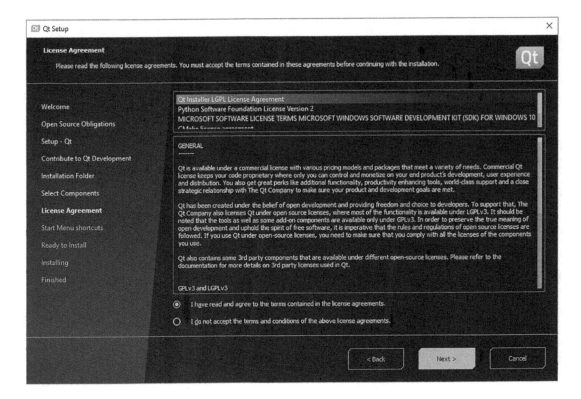

Qt License Agreement Wizard Page

Here you need to agree to the license agreements. If you want to publish your application or code you should read this, as it will tell you what you can and cannot do with the Open-Source license. I recommend contacting the Qt Company when you are unsure about your plans or product.

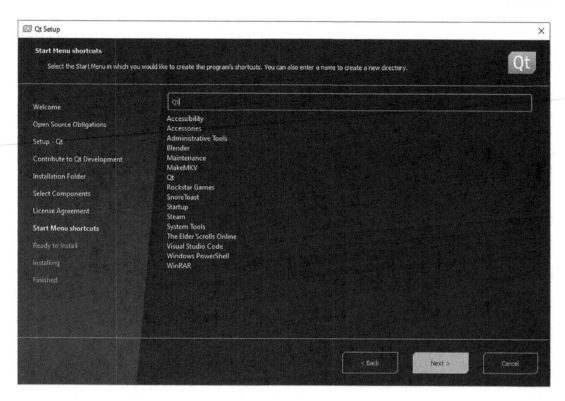

Here you can see that Qt will create a shortcut and integrate it in the window menu, so it can be selected from there.

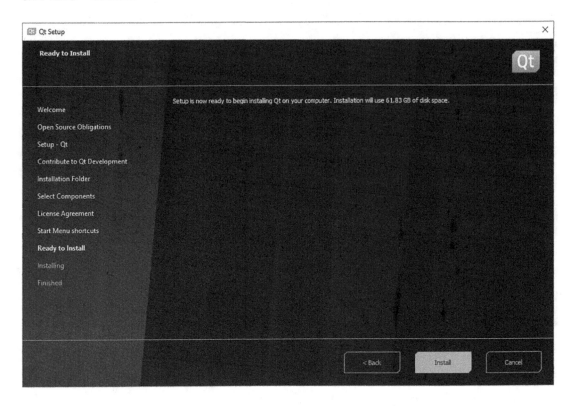

Here Qt tells you how large the installation is going to be. If it is too large for you or you do not have that much space, go back and deselect some of the packages.

Installation page, you can follow the installation here

Now the installation will need to run for quite a while (up to an hour or more, depending on your Internet connection and speed). (Keep in mind that you will most likely never revisit this installer other than to update Qt.) It will install everything you need, and when finished the install button in the bottom right will be enabled.

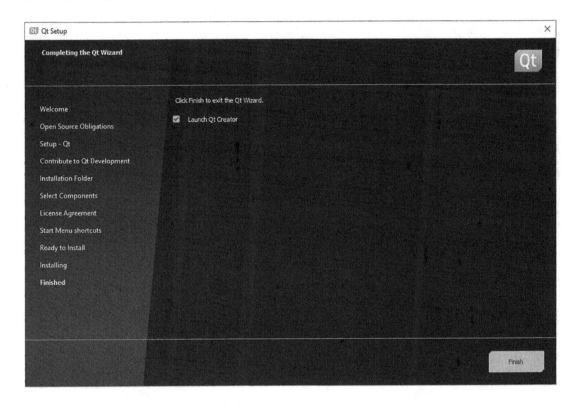

After everything is installed and set up you will be brought to this last page, where you can choose to either open Qt Creator right away or not. Make your choice and then click the Finish button.

Now that you have installed Qt and all the tools belonging to it, you might be wondering how updating and maintaining the software and tools is handled or whether you can download other packages or versions later. This can be done through the Maintenance Tool Qt provides, through which you can manage all the versions and packages on your machine. Qt requires a lot of space and this will only add open time when you install more packages and versions. Depending on the size of the install drive, you might run out of space. For our purposed in this book we will need this again, but the option is there if you need it.

It is worth mentioning that it is not necessary to have multiple versions of Qt on your machine. For this book, you will only work with one version. If you need to work and maintain different software and projects that were made with a different version, then it will be necessary to download and install multiple versions, and I recommend that you update the version related to the software or project.

2.1.2 Downloading and Installing Android Studio

Next, we are going to download and install Android Studio. We will not use Android Studio or the SDKs and NDKs just yet, but it is easiest to run the installations now.

First, locate Android Studio at www.xxx.

Download Android Studio and SDK tools | Android Developers

Android Studio provides the fastest tools for building apps on every type of Android device. Download Not Available. Your current device is not supported. See the ...

Download
版本说明 - 探索Android Studio - Google Play - 预览 - ...

Meet Android Studio
Install - Configure the IDE - Developer workflow basics - ...

Android Studio
Plataforma - Google Play - Documentos - Vista previa - ...

Release notes
SDK Tools - Gradle plugin - Emulator release notes - ...

Google Search of Android Studio

The homepage of Android Studio for Android Developers is not only the place to download the installer we need, but it also provides information on the newest features, the docs, many useful examples and guides to using Android Studio. All of these are essential if you want to use this as your main development environment. For our purposes it is not essential, because we are just using it for the SDK, NDK, and Dev-Tools.

Android Studio provides the fastest tools for building apps on every type of Android device.

DOWNLOAD ANDROID STUDIO

4.1.1 for Windows 64-bit (896 MB)

DOWNLOAD OPTIONS   RELEASE NOTES

Download button for Android Studio

Click the Download Android Studio button, which will open a pop-up where you can read the license agreement and other information. Click the checkbox and the installer will be downloaded.

Download Android Studio

Before downloading, you must agree to the following terms and conditions.

11. LIMITATION OF LIABILITY

11.1 YOU EXPRESSLY UNDERSTAND AND AGREE THAT GOOGLE, ITS SUBSIDIARIES AND AFFILIATES, AND ITS LICENSORS SHALL NOT BE LIABLE TO YOU UNDER ANY THEORY OF LIABILITY FOR ANY DIRECT, INDIRECT, INCIDENTAL, SPECIAL, CONSEQUENTIAL OR EXEMPLARY DAMAGES THAT MAY BE INCURRED BY YOU, INCLUDING ANY LOSS OF DATA, WHETHER OR NOT GOOGLE OR ITS REPRESENTATIVES HAVE BEEN ADVISED OF OR SHOULD HAVE BEEN AWARE OF THE POSSIBILITY OF ANY SUCH LOSSES ARISING.

12. Indemnification

12.1 To the maximum extent permitted by law, you agree to defend, indemnify and hold harmless Google, its affiliates and their respective directors, officers, employees and agents from and against any and all claims, actions, suits or proceedings, as well as any and all losses, liabilities, damages, costs and expenses (including reasonable attorneys fees) arising out of or accruing from (a) your use of the SDK, (b) any application you develop on the SDK that infringes any copyright, trademark, trade secret, trade dress, patent or other intellectual property right of any person or defames any person or violates their rights of publicity or privacy, and (c) any non-compliance by you with the License Agreement.

13. Changes to the License Agreement

13.1 Google may make changes to the License Agreement as it distributes new versions of the SDK. When these changes are made, Google will make a new version of the License Agreement available on the website where the SDK is made available.

14. General Legal Terms

14.1 The License Agreement constitutes the whole legal agreement between you and Google and governs your use of the SDK (excluding any services which Google may provide to you under a separate written agreement), and completely replaces any prior agreements between you and Google in relation to the SDK.

14.2 You agree that if Google does not exercise or enforce any legal right or remedy which is contained in the License Agreement (or which Google has the benefit of under any applicable law), this will not be taken to be a formal waiver of Google's rights and that those rights or remedies will still be available to Google.

☐ I have read and agree with the above terms and conditions

DOWNLOAD ANDROID STUDIO FOR WINDOWS

android-studio-ide-201.6953283-windows.exe

License Agreement of Android Studio and its Tools, especially important that you read this.

If you have done this, then the 600+ MB installer will be downloaded.

Android Studio Installer

Opening the installer and starting the installation displays an opening page with some text about the installer and what is going to be installed, which is for information only.

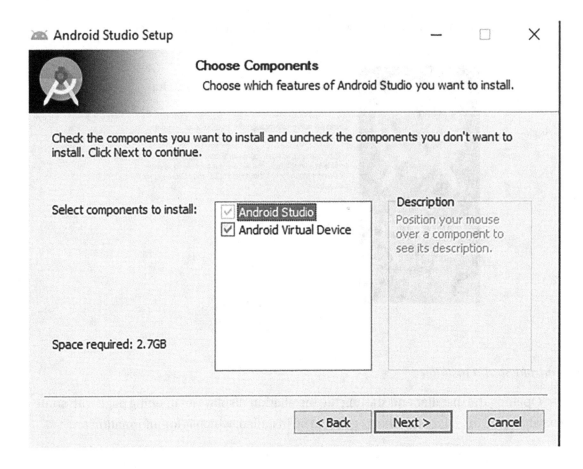

The best choice is to install both Android Studio and Android Virtual Device. The Virtual Device is one of the best features Android Studio comes with, and we will be using it regularly in our Android development. Basically it is an emulator for Android, and a powerful one. There are other emulators available, but they lack the support and the feature specifications of this one.

After choosing which checkboxes to check, then click next and continue.

Choosing the installation path is next, and here you are free to install it wherever you want. I would recommend installing it in a place where you will know where to find it. For me this is my D:\\ drive with a folder on it. Remember that Android Studio must be installed in an empty folder.

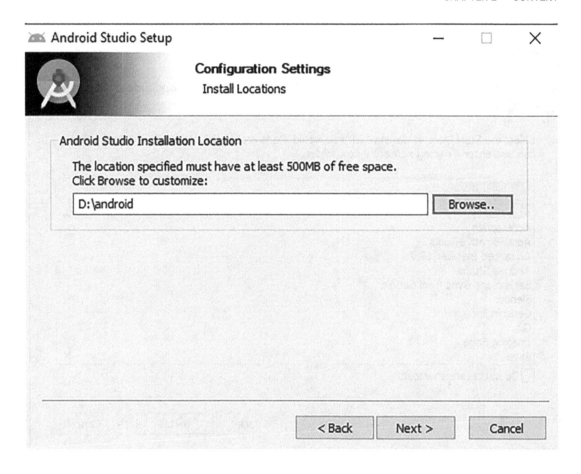

After the installation folder, click next and continue.

Next, we will have the choice of creating a desktop shortcut. I prefer to have one, so I leave it as it is, but if you do not want one then check the box. After this, click next.

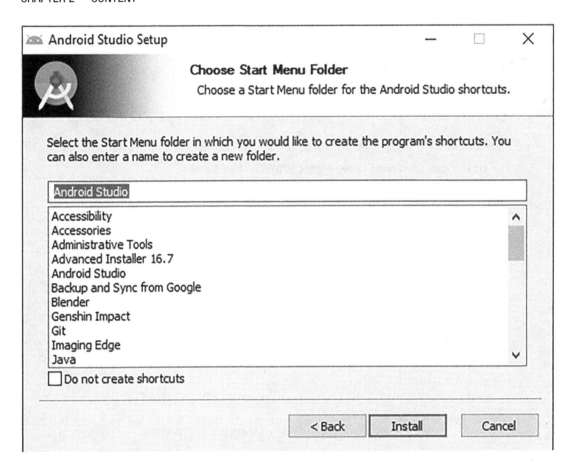

Android Wizard Start Menu and Shortcuts

This will bring us to the progress bar where we can watch the installation take place. You can open the show details button if you would like a better overview of what is being installed at what time. When it is finished, click next and to continue to the last page of the installation.

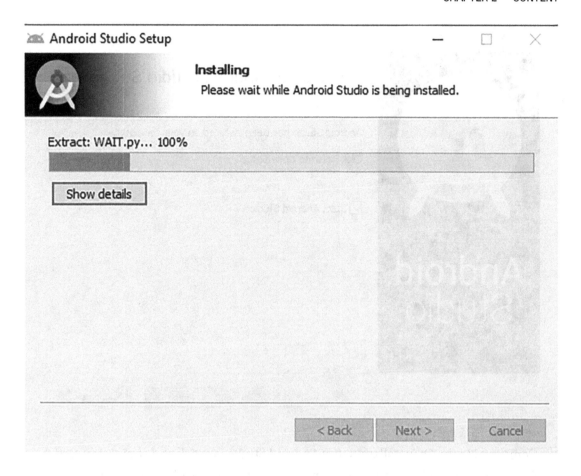

At this point you are finished with the installation and you may open Android Studio if you want to (though you do not need to do so at this time).

Compared to the Qt installation, the Android Studio is quick and straightforward: there are not many options to choose from, and the actual size of the installation is not too large.

In the next section, we will install everything related to Android.

2.1.3 Configuring the Android SDK, NDK, and Development Tools

To configure these tools, we need to open Android Studio.[5] If this is your first time opening Android Studio, you will be presented by the following page:

---

[5] In this book I used Android Studio 4.1.2, but if you have any newer version you should use that one.

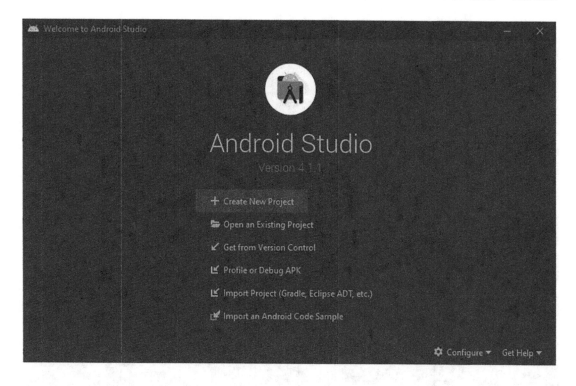

Welcome Page to Android Studio

If you see anything other than this page, or you are required to install something, then follow the on-screen information before returning to the welcome page. Next, open Configure and from there, open the SDK Manager.[6]

---

[6] There are also ways to get there if you have a project open.

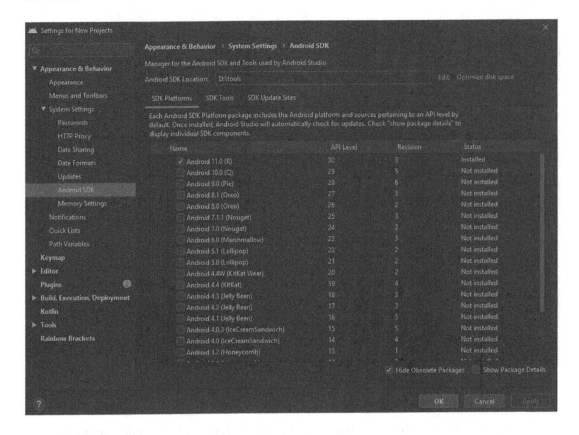

SDK Manager, here you can manage your SDK Platforms and Tools

When you open the SDK Manager,[7] you will be presented with the preceding view. Here we need to do a few things. First, if there is no checkbox active for the newest or any of the SDK Platforms you see open right now, you need to check the box. I recommend opening the most current version, as it will be the most supported version available. I also recommend choosing an older version so that you can test the range of versions your application can work with.

But you should choose a version that is supported by Qt, and that is not very old. I tend to use one or two versions behind the newest version available.

Next, move to the SDK Tools tab up at the top.

_____

[7] The SDK Manger changes from time to time, so do not feel confused when the screenshot does not match what you see here.

Here we need check a few things.

☑ Android SDK Build-Tools		Installed
☑ NDK (Side by side)		Not Installed
☐ Android SDK Command-line Tools (latest)		Not Installed
☑ CMake		Not Installed
☐ Android Auto API Simulators	1	Not installed
☐ Android Auto Desktop Head Unit Emulator	2.0.0 rc1	Not installed
☑ Android Emulator	30.2.6	Installed
☑ Android Emulator Hypervisor Driver for AMD Processors (installer)	1.6.0	Not installed
☑ Android SDK Platform-Tools	30.0.5	Installed
☐ Google Play APK Expansion library	1	Not installed
☐ Google Play Instant Development SDK	1.9.0	Not installed
☐ Google Play Licensing Library	1	Not installed
☐ Google Play services	49	Not installed
☑ Google USB Driver	13	Not installed
☐ Google Web Driver	2	Not installed
☐ Intel x86 Emulator Accelerator (HAXM installer)	7.5.6	Not installed
☐ Layout Inspector image server for API 29-30	5	Not installed

The tools we need

The tools selected are needed, so check to see if they are not visible. If not, check to see if you have disabled hide Obsolete Packages; sometimes Android Studio puts old packages there.

Here is why we need these packages:

- **Android Studio SDK Build-Tools**

  We are going to build Android apps, and for that we need the Build tools.

- **NDK (Side by Side)**

  Qt requires this to build for Android. In the future this may not be the case, but for the time being I strongly suggest always installing it. It is not large and will not take up a lot of space.

- **CMake**

  Qt does not require this to function, but we will be building applications using C++ and it will come in handy.

- **Android Emulator**

  This is one of the best features provided by Android Studio: it is like having your own Android phone on your desktop, and is extremely powerful and great to use. There are problems with it when you want to use it on an PC that has an AMD Processor, but we will cover that later.

- **Android Emulator Hypervisor Driver for AMD Processors (installer)**

  This is required if you have an AMD CPU, as you cannot run Android Emulator without it (unless you use a guide from Google that explains how you need to turn some features on and some off). If you do not have an AMD CPU then you do not need to select this.

- **Android SDK Platform-Tools**

  These are the basic tools need by Android Studio to build, run, and deploy Android applications, and they are also needed for Qt.

- **Google USB Driver**

  If cannot use the emulator or you do not want to, you can also deploy your applications written in Qt or Android Studio to your phone using a USB connection. We will be needing this, so select it.

When you have selected all the packages you want, you then need to change the location where Android Studio downloads and installs these packages. We need to link Qt to these packages, so the best practice is to pick a drive and a folder that you can remember. You should also choose one that does not have any spaces or special characters in it, because these can create problems later in Qt when you want to deploy your application.

If you followed everything we did so far and selected everything I mentioned and selected a suitable folder, you can click OK. This will open a pop-up that lists all the components you want to install. Check to see that everything is as it should be, and then click OK again.

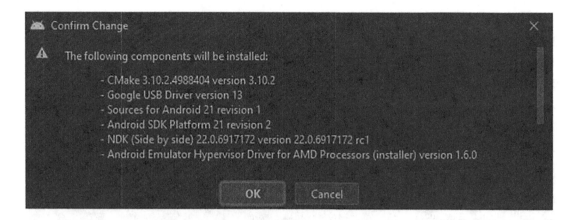

Pop-up with the changes we want

Next you will be bombarded with license agreements, and you need to check all of them. You can only accept these license agreements and terms of use.

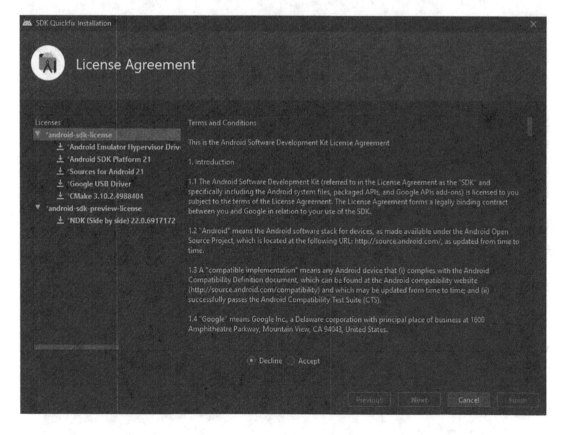

Important License Agreements

There are some interesting points in these agreements, and if you have the time and patience you may want to read up on them. But for our purposes, there is no need to read them. As recommended earlier, you might want to read up on them if you want to publish an application and you are not sure whether what you want to do is acceptable.

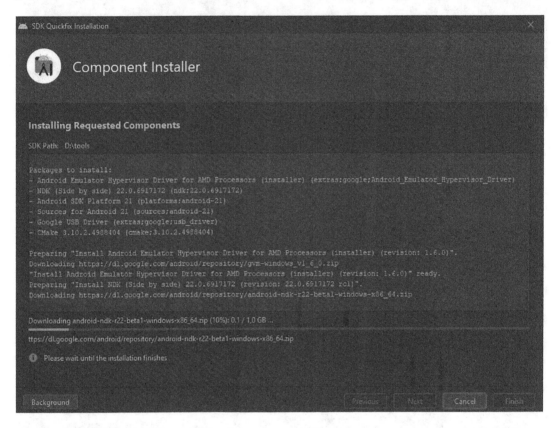

Progress bar of the installation process

At this point the installer will begin, which will download and install all the files you need. Depending on the strength of your Internet connection, this may take a little bit of time.

When the installation has completed you can click Finished, and the SDK Manger will close.

Now we need to link the Android Tools, SDKs, and NDKs to Qt to use them in our development. Open Qt Creator and go to the top bar.

File   Edit   View   Build   Debug   Analyze   Tools   Window   Help

With Qt Creator open, you need to go to Tools. When you hover over it you will be presented with a menu, and from there you can select the last option, which will be the Options.

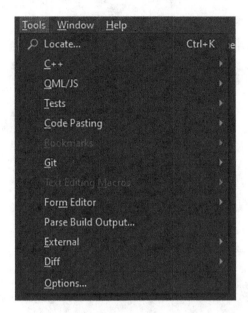

Here you need to go to the Devices tab on the left and open it.

Under Tools there are many good features that you can use in your development. The Git tab is one that I use, and though we are not going to use it this in this book, we are going to set up and use Git Bash.

Device configuration in Qt Creator Settings

Next, you need to go to the Android tab. Here you need to enter the following. First, add the JDK location at the top of the tab.[8]

After that you need to specify the SDK location of our Android SDK. If you successfully set up everything all the items in the drop-down will be checked green, which will complete the installation and linking of the SDKs, NDKs, and tools we need. Sometimes Qt has problems checking for all the files that you have installed, as shown in the preceding screenshot. This is nothing bad. You can still develop your apps like this, and the problem will disappear given enough time.[9]

As a reminder, it is important to always keep the things we just downloaded new and up-to-date. This will minimize the bugs and problems that might occur when developing.

When we are finished with the installation of all the software and setup, we can begin the actual coding.

---

[8] If you do not have JDK on your device, follow one of the tutorials out there or use the guide from my website.

[9] _

2.2 First Steps with Qt

As with any new language or framework, the first thing you will probably do is write a Hello World app, which is what we are going to do here. First, we want to verify that our installation and setup are correct and complete. This will also be a starting point for the main content of this book.[10]

Open Qt Creator, which we have installed on our machine. Click on the New button next to Projects or go to Files and select New Project.

Qt Creator open on Project Tab

Here you can also see your recently opened project, as well as a tab on the left for your examples and tutorials. The marketplace can also be found there.

What you might also see is that generally all Qt projects have a .pro extension that houses all the information about the project, what type it is, the modules used in the project, and so on.

Most interesting in my opinion are the examples and the tutorials, which can greatly add to your knowledge in Qt and help you in learning components and features.

---

[10] If you have followed the steps up to now you are ready to continue, but if you still encounter a problem or are not able to do the next steps then review the last few sections or go to my website bencoepp.io where you can find a link to my Git Hub where you have the files needed to set everything up. This should allow you to at least follow along.

Projects New and Open Button

Selecting New Projects opens a pop-up, which is like a Wizard for creating our project. The steps are not difficult, but for our first time we are going to do this together. It will also be covered in more detail in a later section, where I go over more crucial steps in setting up a project that are not necessary to know right now.

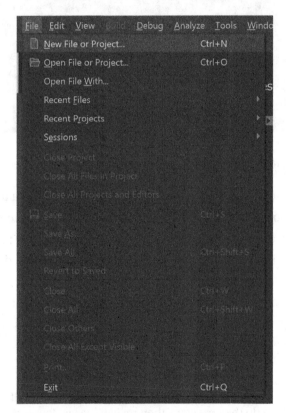

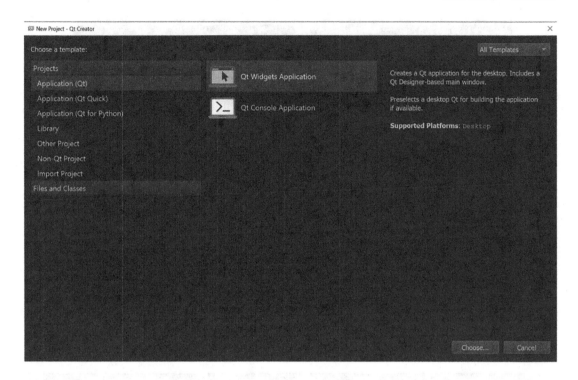

New Project Wizard

The first thing you will see when the Wizard opens is the different project templates that Qt provides.[11] Some of them are not as useful as others, but I will point out the ones that are worth remembering.

Generally, you can say that a template is equal to a application.

---

[11] There are many very specialized templates that you can check out, and if you find something that fits your workflow then you can use it.

Creates a Qt application for the desktop. Includes a Qt Designer-based main window.

Preselects a desktop Qt for building the application if available.

Supported Platforms:

- Android Device
- Desktop
- WebAssembly Runtime
- Windows Runtime (Local)

This is the first of the Qt applications.

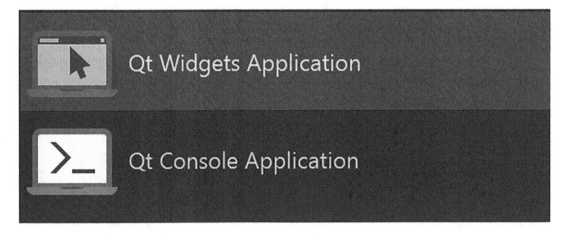

Application (Qt)

These are the standard Qt C++ Applications you can find. The first is a Widget Application, which is a basic and native GUI application that provides a style file and a C++ backend for development. The one below that is a Console Application, which has all the things included that you would need to build a terminal or console application.

I have used the latter multiple times in building my own Git Terminal and a simple Tetris game in C++, as well as a snake game. But its most useful purpose is not with games, but with developer and workflow-related tasks.

If you wanted to go into learning about the C++ functionality Qt has to offer, this would be the template I would choose. As Qt is a C++ framework, you can expect there to be a lot of power and functionality under the hood. And if you want to truly master and understand Qt and all of its aspects, you will also need to learn the C++ side of Qt.[12]

Next is the Qt Quick Application.

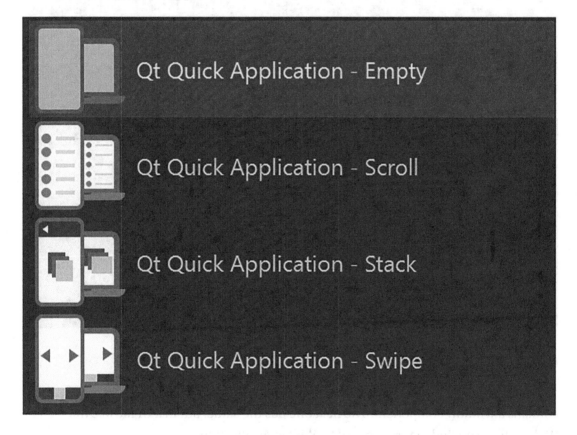

Application (Qt Quick)

Here you have a three wide and especially useful project templates, including the Scroll and Swipe templates. These are excellent for trying out these functionalities or adding to them, which you are going to do all the time because they are one of the most

---

[12] We will not be covering this in here in this book. There are a lot of great tutorials as well as learning resources out there how to do this.

essential components Qt provides. The Stack template is also useful, but for the way I use Stack View most of the time not usable. There is also an Empty Qt Quick Application. It comes with all the elements and files that make up the most basic working Qt Quick Application, and for me is always the starting point for a new project.

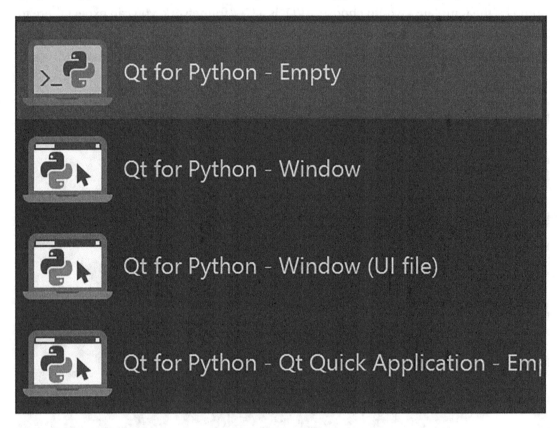

Qt for Python Templates

Next are the Python templates, the first of which is an empty project that only contains a window component. The next one has the same, but in a UI file like the Widgets files you find in the standard Qt Widget Applications.

Lastly, we have the basic Empty Qt Quick Application in the Python version. It is nearly identical to the Qt Quick version but has a C++ backend instead of a Python one. If you are someone who is used to Python, you can jump right into it here.

Finally, there are some quite different but always useful templates. There are multiple different options for cloning a project from a Version Control System, such as Git. I usually do not use these, but I know they are useful for many (and they can save you from opening a terminal).

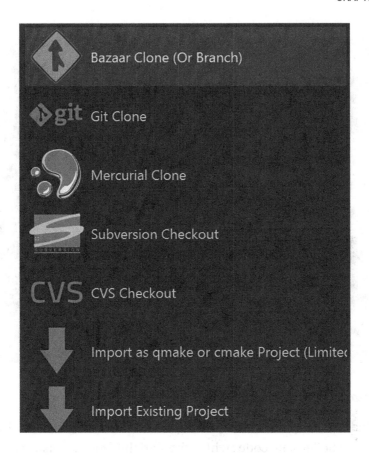

VSC Templates

At the bottom, there are the two options for opening an existing project.

We want to choose Qt Quick Application, since it is the best way of making applications with Qt (and in my opinion the best way of building any application regardless of the framework you are using). It is the most recent, very feature-rich, and has all the functionality you need to make any application possible. In Qt Quick Applications you mainly write the UI (User interface) using QML, a language mainly used in Qt. It allows the creation of highly stylized and animated UIs and applications. Because it is my favorite thing to program with, which you will be hearing quite a bit about it throughout the book.

Next, we have the choice between several different templates. For our Hello World application the best option is the Empty template,[13] so click Choose.

---

[13] We do not require anything in terms of prebuild components, but if you want to you can see what the other templates have to offer.

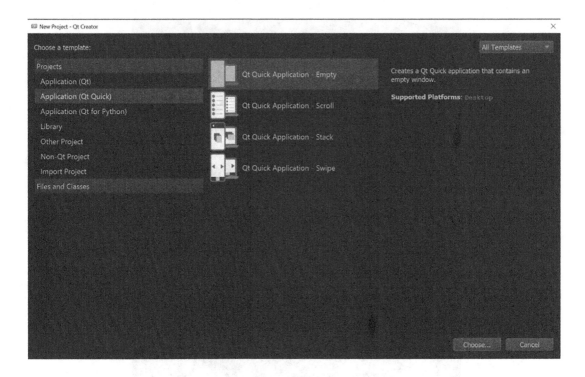

New Project Wizard QtQuick Templates

Keep in mind that templates are not as important as you might think. They provide you with a bit more boilerplate code right at the start, but you can also create this on your own in just a few minutes of work. But if you are a beginner, then a quick look into how these templates work and how they use the components can be a particularly good learning experience.

When you continue, you can choose the project location. This is an important step of the setup.

Choosing the name of the project is the easiest part, and this is totally up to you. I recommend against having any spaces or special characters in the name, and this also extends to the location you save it in. This is not as crucial as it used to be, but with a few earlier versions of Qt there was a problem that you were too able to deploy your application using windeployqt.[14] This is why I recommend avoiding spaces or special characters. But if you just want to develop an application or you are not interested in deploying it, then feel free to name and place it wherever you want.

---

[14] This is a tool created by the Qt Company that helps developers deploy applications to the Windows platform.

After you type a name for your app and select the location where you want to save it, click the Next button and continue.

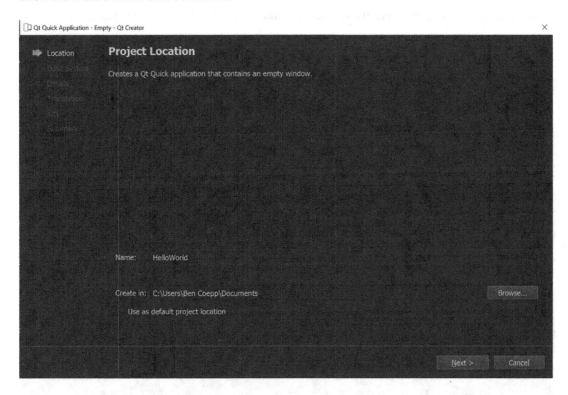

Project Location Page in New Project Wizard

Choosing the Build system is a crucial step in a creating a new application. You have the option between qmake,[15] CMake,[16] and Qbs. Each has their separate reasons for use, depending on your type of applications you want to make. In later sections we are going to talk about the different benefits for using one over the other.

Build system:	qmake	
	CMake	
	Qbs	

Different Build System Qt provides

---

[15] A utility that automates the generation of makefiles tailored to the platform where it is run from.

[16] Cross-platform free and open-source software for build automation, testing, and packaging using a compiler-independent method.

Here we are going to use qmake, but all other options are also viable. (CMake is also a good choice, as we are building C++ applications and CMake is one of the standard build systems to use.) But here we will use qmake as it is the standard and default.

New Project Wizard Build System

Next, we need to select the Qt versions we want to use. In general, you should always use the newest version available. For us, this is Qt 6.[17]

Below the version you have the option to use the Qt Virtual Keyboard. Right now it is not needed, so leave it unchecked and click Next.

---

[17] As of time of writing this book it is the newest version available. If you have a newer version then use that, but it is not as important as you might think. The content in this book regardless of the version you are running.

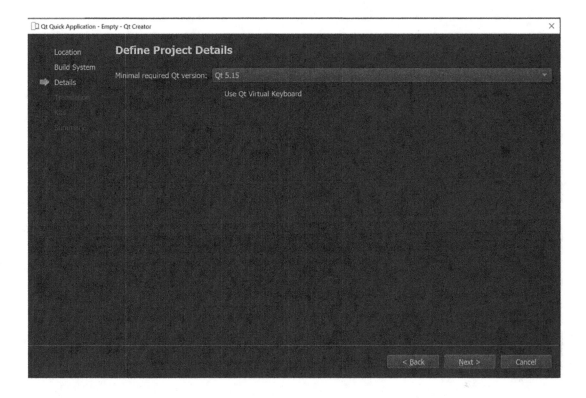

For some reason, the minimal required Qt Version is Qt 5.15, this is also fine, but if you have the option for Qt 6 then choose it

Next, we have the option of adding a translation file. This allows us to give the user the choice between different languages. As users of an application are generally not from the same country, having multiple languages can be especially useful. But right now it is not needed, so we are going to skip this. Click Next and continue.

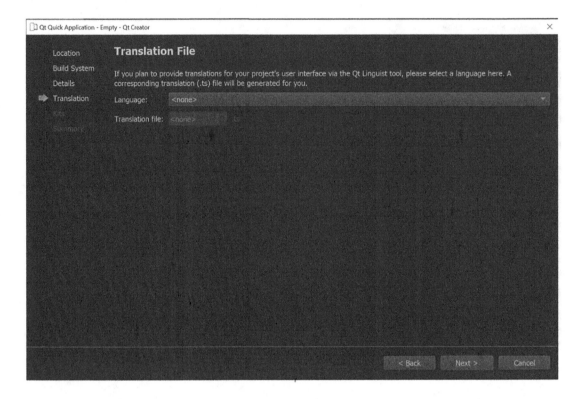

Kits are the different platforms you can build your application for. For our purposes we will be building it on desktop, but there are many more platforms out there, such as UWP, Android, MSVC, and Apple/IOS. Later in the book we are going to use a lot of different kits, but right now we are only using the MinGW 64-bit/32-bit kit. It is the basic kit for developing desktop applications. Once you have selected it, click Next and continue.

Note that if you are on Mac or Linux you can also choose another kit, but we will be sticking to MinGW 64-bit for most of the tutorials and content in this book.

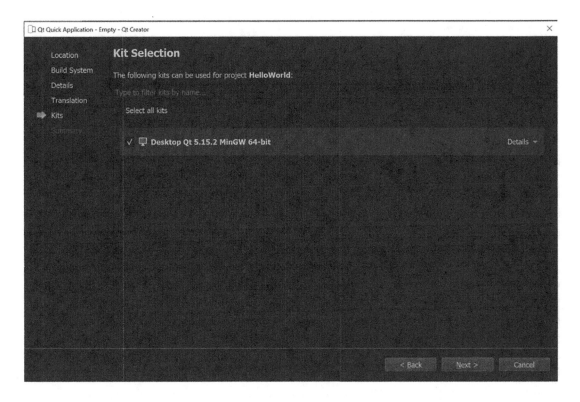

New Project Wizard Kit *Selection*

Finally, you have the option of adding a Version Control System to your project.

This will be an especially useful thing in the future, and if you build anything larger than a calculator that can be built in a few days, you should use one. There are many reasons for adding a Version Control System, because you can keep track of all your changes and edits and even if you destroy your entire project, you can revert to a functioning version of your application.[18]

Later I will explain how to use this and how to set it up. But for our tiny Hello World application we do not need Version Control, so click Finish.

---

[18] I completely destroyed some applications I had written and I did not have VCS on them, so the entire application was more or less completely lost, which was a real shame. So be aware that if you do not use this, you will have a hard time getting your application back if you deleted it or even worse, broke it.

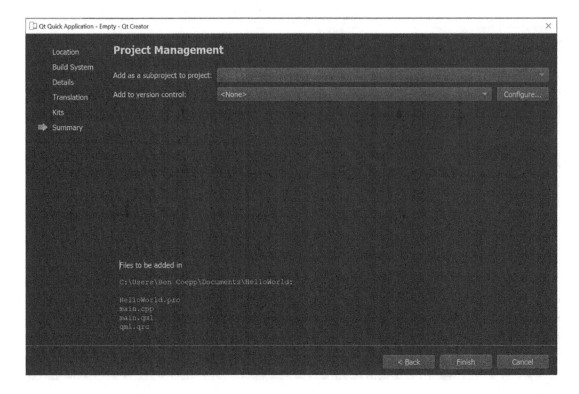

New Project Wizard Project Management

Here you can see the files that are going to be created when you click Finish. We will review the created files later.

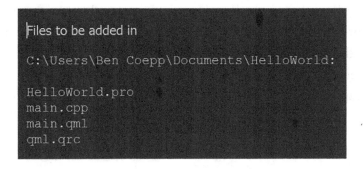

When you click Finish the project is created, and it will be opened. Next, we are going to look at what was created and how everything works.

If you have larger project setups or have multiple subprojects, then you can see here how many files you created, the names of the files, and the type of files.

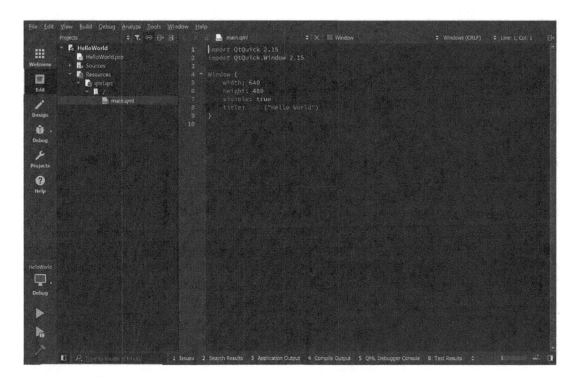

View of an Open Project in editor tab

Now that we have a project, we run it. There is no sense in programming an application if it will not even run. To test to see if it runs, click on the green Arrow in the bottom left.

If you do not want to debug your application, then click the button without the little bug beside it. If everything works out fine and all the setup we did was correct and functional, then the application will run and a window will pop open.

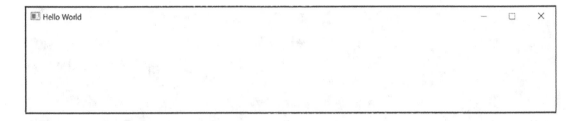

Running Hello World application

For now it is only an empty window with a title that says Hello World: nothing fancy, but the perfect starting point to learn from.[19]

2.3 Explaining the Basics

Now that we have everything set up and we have created our first Hello World application, we should have a look at how a Qt application works and what each part means.

2.3.1 Project Structure

There are many ways of handling project structure, and we are going to go over all the common and recommended ways as well as some that have their benefits in specific cases.

Generally, Qt apps are structured as follows. At the top you have the .pro file, which is like the project settings file and the basic controlling file that handles the building of the project.

---

[19] As a side note, people often use Hello World applications to start off as their first program because it was one of if not the first program ever run by humans. It is also the simplest program you can create. The only function of a Hello World program is to display Hello World: it is precise, simple, and you can immediately test to see if your application runs. It will also teach you the fundamentals of the programming language you want to learn.

Below that you have your sources. Here you will find all your C++ files, scripts, and the like. In an empty project there will only be a main.cpp file in it. This is the heart and soul of a Qt application. This is the link between our qml files and the C++ backend that does the actual displaying of our application.

Content of main.cpp

```
1.    #include <QGuiApplication>
2.    #include <QQmlApplicationEngine>
3.
4.    int main(int argc, char *argv[])
5.    {
6.    QCoreApplication::setAttribute(Qt::AA_EnableHighDpiScaling);
7.
8.        QGuiApplication app(argc, argv);
9.
10.       QQmlApplicationEngine engine;
11.       const QUrl url(QStringLiteral("qrc:/main.qml"));
12.       QObject::connect(&engine, &QQmlApplicationEngine::objectCreated,
13.                        &app, [url](QObject *obj, const QUrl &objUrl) {
14.           if (!obj && url == objUrl)
15.               QCoreApplication::exit(-1);
16.       }, Qt::QueuedConnection);
17.       engine.load(url);
```

```
18.
19.        return app.exec();
20.    }
```

For now it contains only the default setup, which launches the QQmlApplicationEngine and gives it our main.qml file as its starting point. This is all that you can really see of the Qt backend; the rest we will review later, but for now you only need to remember that you probably will not need to go in here at all and if so, it would only be to add or change one or two lines. The rest can be left as it is.

Below our sources you will find the resources.

Empty qml.qrc Folder

This is the place where you will find the actual files of your application. Here you will place your QML files that make up your app as well as images, icons, and JavaScript files. In general, everything that makes up your app goes here.

For people who want to know a bit more, the minimum code required to run a Qt application looks like this:

```
1.    #include <QApplicaiton>
2.
3.    Int main(int argc, char **argv){
4.    QApplication app (argc, argv);
5.    Return app.exec();
6.    }
```

This is all you need to get your Qt application running with the minimum of required code.

2.3.2 App Structure

App structure is less about the files and how they are organized and more about how you use them and work with them. As already mentioned, you will work most of your time inside the resources folder, which houses all your files and the like. This should also be clearly divided between QML files, images and icons, and JavaScript files. Why? Well, if you make anything larger than a calculator, you will most likely have over 10 QML files and even more other data, which can be very overwhelming and confusing if they are not organized and structured.

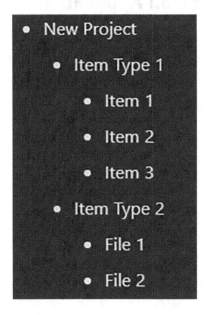

There are two main methods behind doing this. One is to make the organization and structure through the file types. This can be helpful if you do not have a very component- or page-based application, but it can also result in having hundreds of QML files unordered in one place. For this reason this method may not be the best option, but there are companies out there that use nonexisting project structures and just dump all their files of one type into a folder.

The other method is to use a more component and element-based approach. It works by packing everything that is needed for one specific element, page, or section into one folder. This can be extremely helpful, as it is quite easy to understand which files belong to which element in your app, but depending on how large your application gets you will have hundreds or thousands of elements and components. A good example of this would be Instagram, where you have sometimes up to a thousand posts in one list, and if you do not manage your components correctly and keep the resource needs in check, the user will have a frustrating and overwhelming experience. I still prefer this option, however, as it is easy to get into and if you stick to it will make your life a little easier.

But regardless of which structure you prefer, we are going to use both in this book because there is no inherently better way, and if you want to be a professional Qt developer you should probably be familiar with both methods.

2.3.3 How Qt Creates an Application

QML files are like a blueprint for Qt Quick Applications. When you type a component into it with all the necessary elements, Qt parses them and presides to display them. Here in our main.qml file you can see a single component:

Simple Window component with imports

```
1.    import QtQuick 2.15
2.    import QtQuick.Window 2.15
3.
4.    Window {
5.        width: 640
6.        height: 480
7.        visible: true
8.        title: qsTr("Hello World")
9.    }
```

This Window component is the starting point if you want to make an application that has a window. It has a width and a height as well as a visibility setting and a title. This is standard and easy to understand.

Above the window component you have the imports that are needed for this component to work. You will always use QtQuick in your application, regardless of the size or the specific components you will be using.[20] Below that you find QtQuick. Window, which is a specific QtQuick package that is needed for our window to work. There are a lot of different windows in Qt that all have their own QtQuick import you need to use. But they all work the same way, and each includes the following elements:

---

[20] At least for the common types of application and component it is essential.

- **width**

- **height**

- **visibility**

- **title**

There may also be additional attributes or properties that are used differently, or have a different effect.

This is the simplest application you can make in Qt: a window with a title. As you can see, the actual application is only five lines long, and the lines are descriptive and easy to understand. The best thing about QML is that it is so easy to understand and read, and you do not need to be hassled with a lot of exceedingly difficult abstract topics or words to make a simple window appear. You just type window give it a height, width, and all the other things you need and be done with it.

But if you think this is all you can do with it then you are mistaken. There is always more under the hood.

2.3.4 Structuring Tips and Tricks

Qt is a bit complicated when it comes to organization and structuring, and I would even go as far as saying there is no one correct way of doing it.[21] There is the recommended way, however, which should always be what you try to use when building your applications. There are reasons for using the recommended way.

There is a guide written on the Qt Docs that has many tips, tricks, and best practices for Qt.[22] The guide discusses different topics and concepts in Qt and what to be aware of when building applications. It helped me quite a lot while building larger applications, so I recommend it.

I recommend that you first think before you build your application. It might be true that you can change the structure of your application later, but that takes quite a bit of time and has its own share of problems. So think before you build, and you will not regret it. But that brings me to the second point, which is that you should not be afraid

---

[21] You can find out more under the Qt Docs here: `https://doc.qt.io/qt-5/qtquick-bestpractices.html`.

[22] {AU: Pls. add info re where to find guide here.}

of redoing your structure if necessary. This is especially true if you are working on a large project or something that will be sold or used commercially. It is better to redo something then to make your work difficult and your client unhappy.

2.4 First Real Projects

Just learning about the theory behind everything only brings you so far. Now you might be craving a real project: something to test out Qt and its capabilities.

For that purpose, I will run you through a few apps I have built over the years. They demonstrate a broad overview of all the components in Qt, and I will explain everything as we go. We will be coding step by step, which means you can follow along and code beside me. I will be providing just as much info as we need to build what we want, so if you miss some information or want more, you can go to Git Hub for more details.

This also the perfect time for me to mention the videos on my YouTube channel.[23] There you can find several Qt-related videos on topics such as how I build and program applications in Qt on components that you will use all the time when building applications, including the List-, Stack-, and Swipe Views.

2.4.1 Taskmaster

Whenever I start development in a new language or framework, I start by building this kind of application. What is a Task Master, you ask? This is an application where you can view, add, and delete tasks to a list. This sounds simple, but it requires a lot of functionality that you will use daily in any project.

So we are going to start out with this. Let's jump right in.

2.4.1.1 Project Creation

Open Qt Creator and create a new project.

---

[23] {AU: Pls. add full URL linking to your YouTube channel here.}

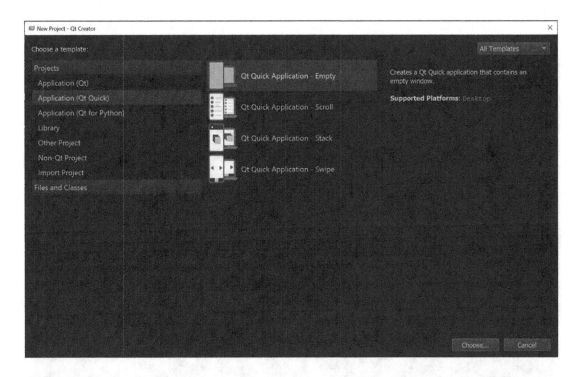

As we did with our practice Hello World application, we are again choosing Qt Quick Application Empty as our template. We could also use the Scroll template this time, as it fits with what we are trying to build, but for ease of use let's stick to the Empty template.

Next we will give our project a descriptive name: TaskMaster. After you type in the name, click Next.

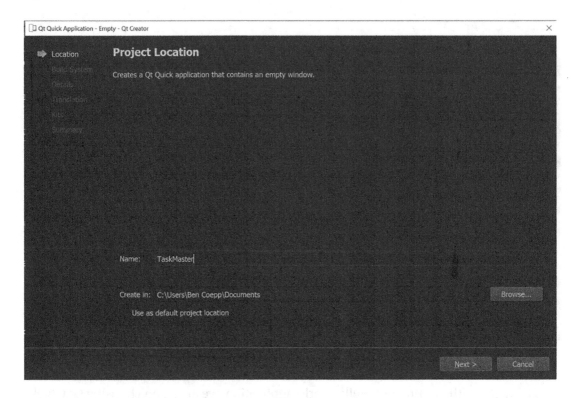

New Project Wizard, pick name and location

The Build System can be left as qmake. As before, we are going to choose the newest Qt version available for us. We do not want a translation file, as we are only doing this app for learning and educational purposes. For the kit we are going to choose MinGW 64-bit or 32-bit. We are only developing the app for teaching purposes, so there is no need for anything else. We also do not need VSC (Version Control System), which we will use in a later project but will skip here. When you are finished click Finish and the project will be created.

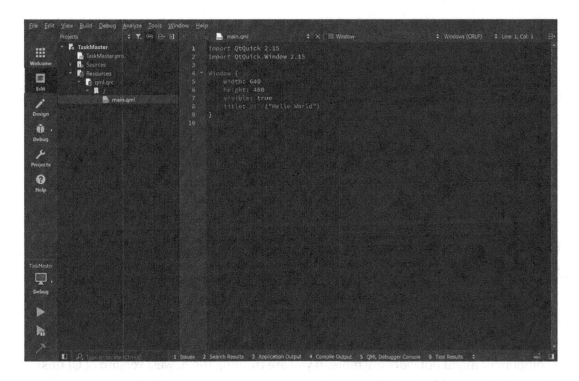

Edit Page after Project creation

As you can see, we are now at the exact same point as we were in our Hello World application.

The first thing I always do when starting a new project is updating the imports in the main.qml file. For whatever reason Qt does not create the QML Files with the newest imports, so let us change that.

Qt imports

```
1.    import QtQuick 2.15
2.    import QtQuick.Controls 2.12
3.
```

Currently we have QtQuick 2.15 and QtQuick.Window 2.15 as our imports in our main.qml file. QtQuick 2.15 is the newest version available, so we can leave it as it is, but we do not need QtQuick.Window. What we need is QtQuick.Controls 2.12,[24] which

---

[24] These are in my opinion essential for QtQuick applications that provide you with the basic functionality you will need. Also, QtQuick.Controls 2.12 is the newest version available to me.

is more or less essential for most Qml applications as it has all the basic controls and functionality that you will need to build most applications.

If you changed both you will have this in your file:

```
1.    import QtQuick 2.15
2.    import QtQuick.Controls 2.12
3.
4.    Window {
5.    width: 640
6.    height: 480
7.    visible: true
8.    title: qsTr("Hello World")
9.    }
```

You might get an unknown component, (M300), which will typically happen if you do not have the current packages imported or the component is not spelled properly. In this case we deleted the QtQuick.Window package from our imports, so window as a component might not work anymore. If you are running the newest version of Qt this should not be a problem, but if you get this error then you know why.

Simple Boiler Plate ApplicationWindow

```
4.    ApplicationWindow {
5.    width: 640
6.    height: 480
7.    visible: true
8.    title: qsTr("Hello World")
9.    }
```

We are going to use ApplicationWindow, which is basically just like our window; I just prefer it as it has some nice capabilities under the hood that the window does not have. But in this case, it does not really matter that much what window you are using. Next we are going to change the title of our application. Currently it says Hello World, but here we will change it to something more fitting.

Titel property of our ApplicationWindow

```
8.    title: "Task-Master"
```

As you can see, I also deleted the qsTr ("") from line 8. Why? Well, qsTr is a lovely thing Qt has under the hood, an internationalization tool. You can add this to any title and text attribute that a component might have, and if a user from another country uses your app, you can specify a translation of that text using the translation files Qt provides. This is extremely useful when you want to build applications that you are going to publish worldwide.

Most commonly you will find that there are two or more languages used in translation. You have a primary language that is the main focus in development (most likely the native language of the developers), and then you have two other primary languages (such as English, French, or Mandarin) that will make it more or less possible for nearly all people on the planet to understand what you have written.

In our case it is not necessary, as we do not want to translate our application to any other language then English.

2.4.1.2 Loading the Pages

Now to the first component we are going to write in our application, a Stack View. With this Stack View we want to change the page when we load all our data. The Stack View will have an initial item that is our loading page, and in our loading page we are going to load all the data we need for our application. If this is a success, then we are going to switch to our main content page. This is the easiest way of making a loading page work in Qt.

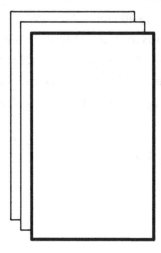

The easiest way of imagining Stack View is to think of several pages stacked behind each other, where you can change the page in front of that stack.

It is one of the most commonly used components for a variety of reasons, in our case for loading another page. You can also load remote pages or images through this feature.

First, type out Stack View with the corresponding brackets.

```
1.  import QtQuick 2.9
2.  import QtQuick.Controls 2.5
3.
4.  ApplicationWindow {
5.  width: 360
6.  height: 720
7.  visible: true
8.  title: "Task-Master"
9.
10. StackView{
11.
12. }
13. }
```

After that add the id to our Stack View. Here I am choosing contentFrame for our id, mainly because this is the frame where all our content will be brought.

The id of a component is like its name, an it must always be unique. You can call the id of a component from anywhere in the QML File it originates from and if you import this file in another qml file, you can call it there too. This calling of ids gives you the ability to also call the attributes from the component as well as the functions and methods belonging to it. The best comparison I was able to come up with was that of ids in HTML documents. They are also unique names for components and make it possible to interact with the corresponding component through the id.

```
1.  import QtQuick 2.9
2.  import QtQuick.Controls 2.5
3.
4.  ApplicationWindow {
5.      width: 360
6.      height: 720
7.      visible: true
8.      title: "Task-Master"
9.
```

```
10.        StackView{
11.            id: contentFrame
12.        }
13.    }
14.
```

With the id written, let us add the next attribute we need. Currently our component does not have a width and a height. We could now just give it a static width and height, but this leads to problems when the user resizes the window, so we are going to use anchors.

Anchors are as the name suggests: they anchor the component corresponding to the point you specify. For us, the best anchor will be this:

```
12.    anchors.fill: parent
```

We can use this to fill our parent, the ApplicationWindow with our Stack View. This could also be done using this:

```
12.    width: parent.width
13.    height: parent.height
```

This is also totally acceptable, and is just two lines except for one. Also, when using anchors.fill you also position the element at 0, 0 on the screen. This is not the case with width and height as I show here; it is true that it also positions itself on 0, 0 but this could also change, and with an anchor changing the position is only possible when using a margin intentionally. In this instance chose the preceding option.

There is a use for using the second option, which is when you import a page from another qml file. There the anchor option confuses Qt. That does not mean it is not going to work, but you are going to get some warnings about not using anchors in that instance and I would recommend not using them there.

qrc:/Main/Load_Page.qml:4:1: QML Load_Page: StackView has detected conflicting anchors. Transitions may not execute properly.

You may see warnings like this, but you can more or less ignore them, unless you encounter a real problem when using it.

Next, we need to set the initialItem for our Stack View. This is going to be our Load Page.

```
13.    initialItem: Qt.resolvedUrl("")
```

This is all we need to add. Between the "" we are going to place the URL for our Load Page, after we create it.

If you added everything so far, we can move onto the next point, creating the Load Page.

Note that we will tend to create a lot of pages throughout these examples, so refer to this section if you need to create a new page and you do not remember how to do this.

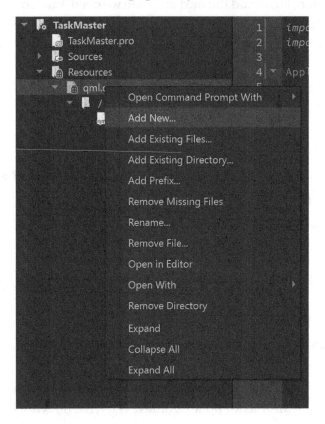

Adding new Files

Go over to the left where the project tree can be found. There you need to right-click on qml.qrc. This will open a menu where you find Add New, and when you click this a wizard will open.

C/C++ File Wizard

This will present you with a similar wizard for creating a new project. First you need to choose what type of file you want to create. The first time you open this wizard up in each project you will be presented by the C/C++ templates. These will be important, but not right now.

We need a QML file. For that, go over to the left and chose Qt.

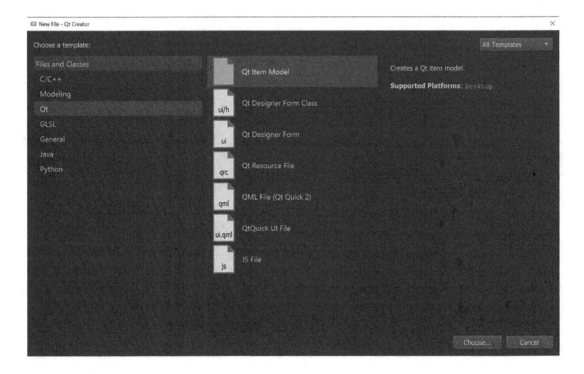

Qt File Wizard

This houses a lot of the files you will be using daily, such as qrc resource files for organizing your files and project structure, QML files and QtQuick UI files that serve the same purpose of being the elements that make up the UI of a Qt Quick Application, and JS files.

As you can see there are a lot of different files and file types here, and they all have their select usage. Some are a little easier to understand, such as JavaScript. If you need to write a lot of JavaScript functionality or you have several functions that you do not want to have in your UI, then this is a perfect option. This also extends to qml files, as they are what we are using for the UI Elements, but some other files like qrc or ui.qml files are a little harder to understand.

My advice is that you look up their respected uses on the Qt Docs and then see if you need it. I do not use many of these files; most of the time just Qml, JavaScript, and maybe qrc when I really need to.

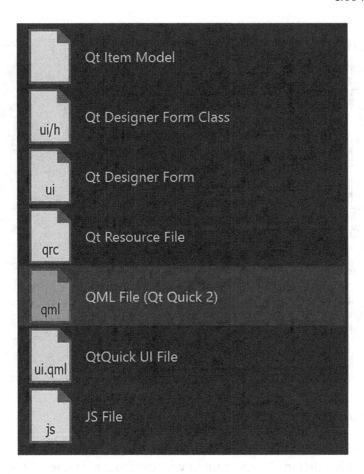

We want the QML file, so select it and click Choose. This will bring you to the next page in the wizard where you need to give the file a name and a location. In this case I will name the file Load_Page. You could also use CamelCase, but I prefer to separate the name of the file and what type of component it is through a _.

That is just my preference, and you can always choose to use another naming scheme, but remember that you need to keep that naming scheme for the entire project.

There is nothing more frustrating than trying to understand one's code when the naming scheme changes midway through. So remember to keep one for one project.

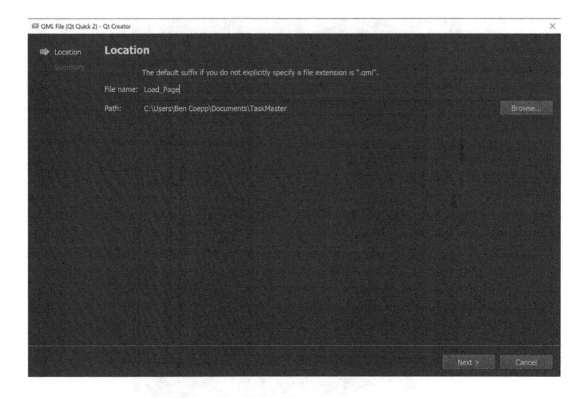

New Project Wizard Project Location

You might also choose the path where the file is saved, which can be helpful if you have an already existing file structure or you want to create one. My way of doing it mostly consists of having all files related to one component in one folder, which is particularly good if you view the project structure, but it takes a few extra steps to set up.

In our app here we will not change the location; just the default location is sufficient. As a side note, the default location will always be the root folder of your application.[25]

When you have decided on the name and the location, click next.

---

[25] This might not be that great depending on how many files you have; if you have over 15 you might want to add folders in which you place your files to minimize the clutter that the files create.

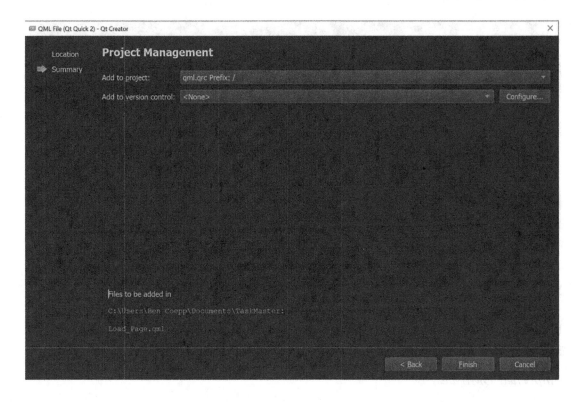

Add to Project Management Wizard

On the last page in the wizard, you will have the choice to add the file to a Version Control System if you have it active for the project. You can also choose which prefix you want to add the file.

Mainly this is the summary page, where you can see what is going to happen and what files are being created. When you are done click Finish, and this will create the file in our project.

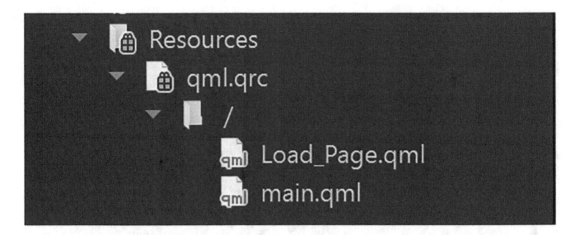

As you can see here, the Load_Page.qml was added right above our main.qml file. If you want, you can always choose to move the file later.

Try to keep the project tree as clean and organized as you can. Depending upon how big your project becomes, having an unorganized project tree can really hinder your ability to work.

Empty new QML file

```
1    import QtQuick 2.0
2
3    Item{
4
5    }
6
```

If you open our newly created file there is not a whole lot to look at just yet. One of the first things you might realize is that the QtQuick import is completely out of date, so change this to:

```
1    import QtQuick 2.15
```

We are also going to add QtQuick.Controls to our project.

```
1    import QtQuick.Controls 2.12
```

I wish Qt would always use the Qt imports we have in our main.qml as a base for all future files, but I can understand that this a little hard to implement and it makes no real difference in most cases. You just need to remember to update and add this to every new file you create.

Currently the item inside our Load_Page.qml has no width as well as no height. So let's add that.

```
1    width: parent.width
2    height: parent.height
```

As mentioned already, in a few steps we will fill the parent of this item with the item itself. This is a genuinely nice way of keeping the same aspect ratio and display size in all our components.

With the creation of the page out of the way, let us get the page displayed on screen. For that you need to go back into our main.qml file and change the initial item of our Stack View to the URL of our Load_Page.

You can get the URL by right-clicking on the file in our project tree and selecting Copy URL.

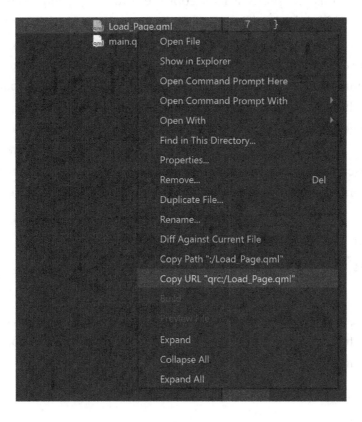

Copying URLs

This will save the URL to your clipboard, and we can paste it inside of the initial item of our contentFrame.

Simple Load- and Main Page Stack View setup

```
10    StackView{
11      id: contentFrame
12      anchors.fill: parent
13      initialItem: Qt.resolvedUrl("qrc:/Load_Page.qml")
14    }
```

It might be important to mention that you do not need the *qrc:/* in front of the URL here. As our Load_Page.qml is inside of the same directory and Prefix as the main.qml, this means that you could just write Load_Page.qml here. I always keep it in even when it is in the same directory and prefix as I just copy the URL; also, when you have a different project structure with multiple different prefixes or even multiple different qrc resource directories, you will need to use the full URL as we did here.

With that we are done with the Stack View in our main.qml. If you were now to start up the application, you would be greeted by nothing. The Load_Page is loaded, but the problem is that there is currently nothing in our Load_Page. So let's change that.

First we are going to make a background for our Load_Page. There are a few ways we could do this. We can change the item tag to a page tag and then add a background attribute. Or we can add a rectangle and make it as big as the item (this is my preferred option). It is a remarkably simple, easy-to-understand, and usable option, so let us do that.

```
8    Rectangle{
9      id:bgRec
10    }
```

We are going to give this an id: this might not be necessary right here, but it is a good practice to have telling ids for everything. You might never know when you might need to get the id of a component you have.

```
10    anchors.fill: parent
```

For the width and the height, we are going to use anchors again, as with the Stack View. This is mainly because I want to save us another line to write, and because here it is the more suitable and elegant solution to the problem.

The last thing to do is give the rectangle a color. I have my color set, so we are going to use the colors I have picked. If you want to use your own feel free to do so. And if you want to get my color sheet, you can find it in my Git Repository for this project.

```
11    color: "#2C3E50"
```

As I am not a designer, I am not interested in creating a stunning and beautiful app. For me it is all about the functionality.

A simple background will not do the trick for a Load_Page, so we need to add some sort of Busy Indicator. We could now create our own Busy Indicator that would have a nice animation, our we could just use the one provided by Qt.

To get the Load Indicator working on our Load_Page we could now just type it out, but I would rather use the Designer. As it is our first time using it, it can be somewhat overwhelming, so read carefully.

Opening the Designer is not hard; if you have opened our Load_Page you can go the left where the sidebar is located. Here you will find the Design button.

Click on the Design tab and the Qt Designer will open. Depending on how large the QML file is and how many different components are inside of it, this can take a little bit of time.

There are also a lot more tabs that might interest you. First is the project tab, where you can edit the kits you have as well as the build systems that are available.

The Debug tab can also be extremely helpful as you can find problems, bugs, and other things through the Debug View. Lastly we have the Help tab, where you can find information on Qt components and features. You can also open the Qt Docs through here, so you might want to look at it when you are lost.

When Qt Designer opens you will be presented with the View, which you can see in the next screenshot.

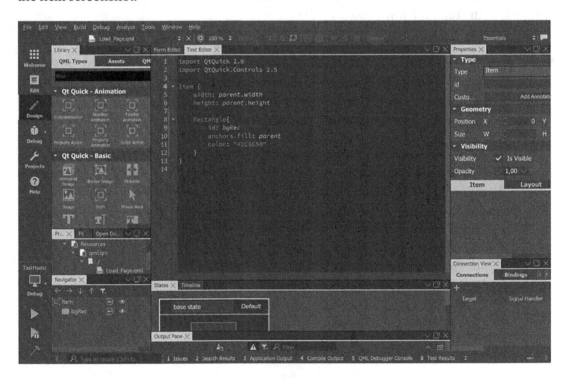

Do not be overwhelmed by all the input you see. The first thing we are going to is switch to the Form Editor. This can be done right above our Text Editor. There you have the Form Editor tab. By clicking it, the Form Editor will open.

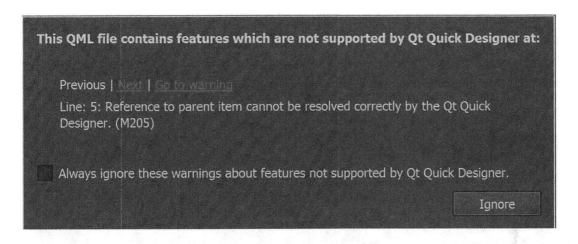

Warning on line 5

Immediately you will be bombarded with a warning. If you were to investigate what this warning stands for, you will find that using patents as a reference to get something works only if there is a parent to the element. We make our item's width and height depending on our parent. Currently this item does not have a parent. This is changed when the file is loaded.

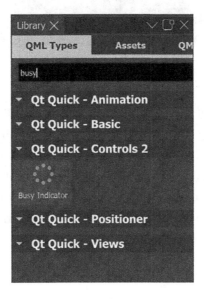

Currently you can ignore this one. You might want to check the box to ignore this all the time, but I would not recommend it. This warning also pops up on other elements inside of our items if there is a break in the parent structure. If you were to ignore this warning, it might lead to you searching endlessly for the problem.

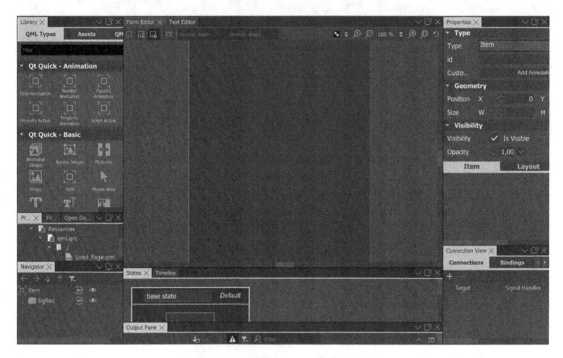

Qt Designer Page

When you click ignore for the warning, you can now see the Form Editor.

The Form Editor is a drag-and-drop designer. You have all the components you currently imported on the left in the Library tab. There you can find anything from the basic animation components and images to labels and buttons. We are going to review where to find what and how to search for something in the Form Editor and Designer later. For now, just type in the search bar under QML types and type in busy indicator.

Now drag and drop the component into the Form Editor and onto our colored background.

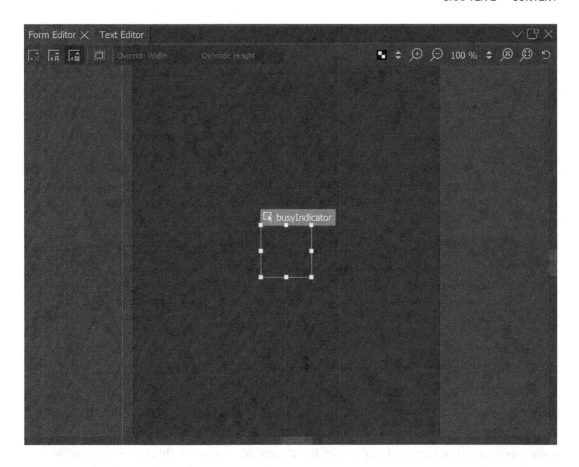

Form Editor close-up

Once you place it there, go back to our Text Editor. You could do this by switching the tab at the top to Text Editor again, but because we are not going to use the Designer right now, let us leave it. Go to the left sidebar and click on Edit, which will bring us back to our normal Text Editor.

If you now investigate our Load_Page.qml you will find that a new Component was added to our file:

```
13    BusyIndicator{
14      id: busyIndicator
15      x: 150
16      y: 290
17    }
18
```

Here we have two new attributes that we have not had so far. These are x and y positions, which are very useful in positioning. The problem arises if you have different types of displays and sizes. If you have fixed x or y positions this will lead to a very unreliable UI and in some cases even break entire applications.

For that reason, we will not be using any fixed x or y positioning but instead use anchors. There are many different anchors out there, but the most used and useful ones are:

- **Anchors.Left**

- **Anchors.Right**

- **Anchors.Top**

- **Anchors.Bottom**

- **Anchors.verticelCenter**

- **Anchors.horizontelCenter**

- **Anchors.centerIn**

These anchors align a component as described, and you can combine them in any way you want. The best way of learning how to use them is by just trying them out.

In this case we will use the anchors.centerIn anchor. We want to center our Busy Indicator on our background in the middle. We could now write this in our normal text editor as we did before, but I want to show you the way you can do this using the Design / Property Editor. Open up the Form Editor again and select the Busy Indicator from the Navigator.

On the right side of our window, you can find a tab called Properties. Here you can edit the properties of all the components you have in our file. This can be very handy when you want to prototype fast, as well as to see what other properties are available.

When you have our Busy Indicator selected, you can see this inside of our Properties Editor:

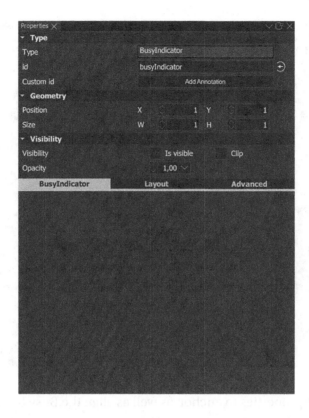

You can see the type and id as well as the size and position of our Busy Indicator. You can also manipulate the visibility from here.

But the most important properties for us are still hidden.

To see them, you need to switch the tab below from Busy Indicator to Layout. This will give you these new properties to play around with:

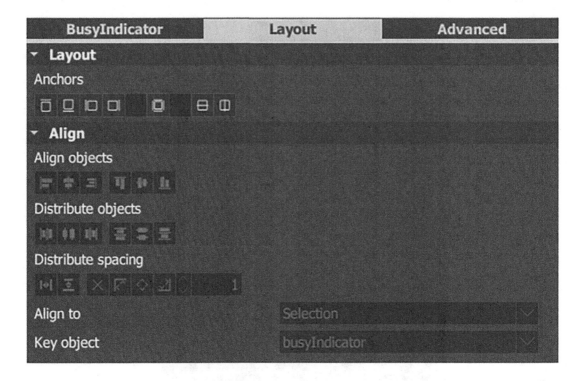

These are all the properties to anchor, as well as align the Busy Indicator in whatever way and shape you want to.

For us, the most important ones are the different anchors at the top. You have all the options from *anchors.right* to the different horizontal and vertical centers. Here you need to just select the *anchors.centerIn: parent*. If you have done that, you are left with this:

```
15    BusyIndicator{
16        id: busyIndicator
17        anchors.fill: parent
18    }
```

Now we are done with our Load_Page. Next is our Main_Page. For that, we are first going to create a new Qml file. We have already done this two times, so you can do it now on your own. If you still need a bit of assistance, then go a few pages back and read up on what to do. The name of the file should be Main_Page and the folder should be the project folder.

When you are done, and the file should be created you are left with this:

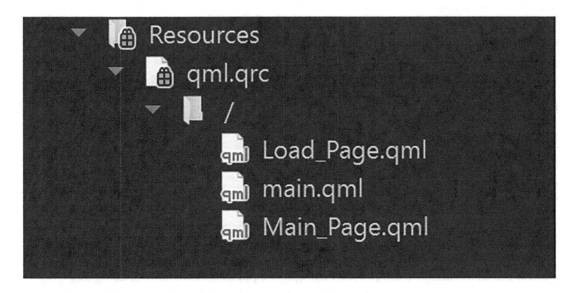

This is a new file in our Project Tree, and if you open the file you will find the standard boilerplate QML file.

Empty new QML file

```
1    import QtQuick 2.0
2
3    Item{
4
5    }
6
```

As before, we need to change the import to QtQuick to 2.15 and add QtQuick. Controls 2.12. If you have a newer version, use that.

New correct imports

```
1    import QtQuick 2.15
2    import QtQuick.Controls 2.12
```

Now we need to add the width and height to our item.

```
5    width: parent.width
6    height: parent.height
```

Next we are going to give our app a proper background to make it a bit easier on the eyes. As this is our first real application, we are only going to use one page and not do anything fancy.

The rectangle itself is the exact same as the one in our Load_Page. Copy it over and place it inside our item.

```
8    Rectangle{
9        id: bgRec
10       anchors.fill: parent
11       color: "#2C3E50"
12    }
```

If you are wondering why we are using the same id for our rectangle, the simple answer is that because we are not importing these pages and we are not using any components in between them, there will not be a problem using the same id. But if you want to be true to form, then use a more telling and unique id.

Currently the page would not change if the app has loaded; it would always stay at the Load_Page. This is not helpful, so let us add the change of pages to our main.qml.

Inside of our main.qml we need to add this to change the pages after loading:

```
16    Component.onCompleted: {
17        contentFrame.replace("")
18    }
```

This code snippet does one simple thing: when the main.qml page has loaded and everything is ready to be rendered on screen, the contentFrame's item will be changed to that of our Main_Page, so our Stack Views items will be changed. Now we only need to place the URL of our Main_Page into the "" and we are done with the replacing of the page when the loading is completed.

```
17    contentFrame.replace("qrc:/Main_Page.qml")
```

With this done, we will next be going over how the app is supposed to work, and then we are going to build it.

2.4.1.3 How the App Works

This is supposed to be a Task Master app, because we want to create and delete tasks. But why do we need to do this? First we need a List View, which will display all the tasks we have created. Next, we need a button that opens up the inputs for us, and lastly, we need a button with which we can submit the inputs.

This is all the functionality we need; it is not much nor is it that complicated. But let me explain a little bit more about what we are doing and how we are going to do this.

The following diagram shows how the application should function and what functionality we need. For this application this would not be necessary as we will not create anything really complicated, but it is better to have a diagram and a plan so that we are not lost while we create the application.

The application works like this: the application starts, and the app loads the List View, which at this point is still empty. Next the user can click the + button, which will then open up our drawer where our inputs are located.

When the user has filled out all the inputs, they can click on the submit button and the drawer is closed again.

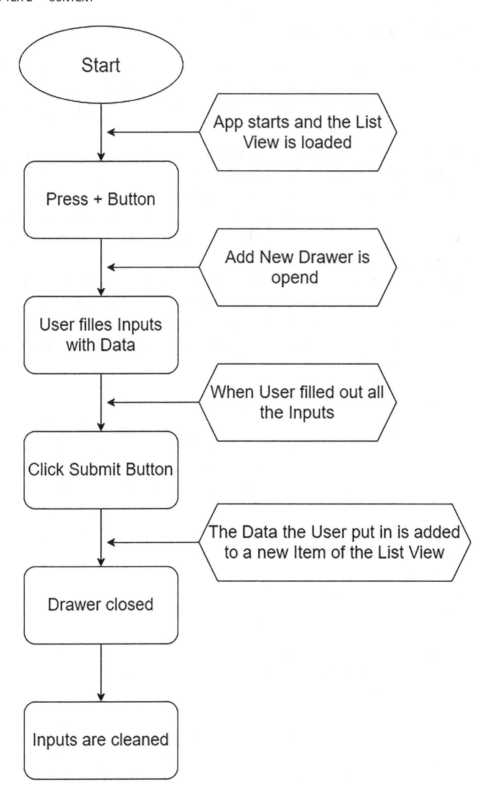

Start

App starts and the List View is loaded

Press + Button

Add New Drawer is opend

User filles Inputs with Data

When User filled out all the Inputs

Click Submit Button

The Data the User put in is added to a new Item of the List View

Drawer closed

Inputs are cleaned

With the click of the Submit button the application takes the data the user has inputted and creates a new List Item from that. With this done, new item is displayed and the inputs are cleaned. Now the user can create a new Item.

2.4.1.4 List View and Displaying Data

As it is now clear what we want to achieve, let us start by building the List View we need. The List View is one of the most important elements of Qt and it is used throughout most applications, so I am going to review it in a bit more detail. First add the List View to our Main_Page.

Empty List View

```
15    ListView{
16
17    }
```

Next our List View needs an id, as well as a width and a height.

```
15    id: listview
16    anchors.fill: parent
```

For the id I choose list view, as it is very descriptive, and we will only need one List View. The width and height will again be handled by *anchors.fill: parent*. It will fill the entire screen, and as we will not have anything else to do in the entire application.

We also need a header and a footer. The header will be our title for the app, and the footer will house our add button. First we are going to write our header.

```
17    header: Item {
18    id: headerListView
19    width: parent.width
20    height: 50
21    }
```

The header attribute requires a component as an input. We are going to give it an Item, with an id, a width that spans the entire screen, and a height of 50. This will be a bar up top that should always stay at the top of our application.

```
22    headerPositioning: ListView.OverlayHeader
```

If we want to have the header always at the top of our List View, we need to add headerPositioning: ListView.OverlayHeader. There are two other ways the Header Positioning can work: the default way of just scrolling with the content as if the header was a normal item, or a header that is pushed up and pulled back when the content is scrolled.

Currently there is nothing inside of our header. Now we are going to add the title. For that we are going to use a Label. This Label comes from QtQuick.Controls and is a simple text element with a few more attributes and abilities under the hood.

```
22   Label{
23   anchors.centerIn: parent
24   text: "Task-Master"
25   color: "black"
26   }
```

For most Labels out there, we need a position where the Label should be, a text indicating what the label should display. We also give the text a color, which is not needed in this instance since Labels have always a default color of black.

With the title out of the way let's add a Model and a Delegate to our List View. These are some of the attributes as well as a width and a height that are essential for a List View.

Models are data, such as an Array, List, or an Array List, and if you know how they work you will also understand Models. Qt has its own data structure under a Model, but fundamentally they work the same as the already mentioned ones. Now let us implement it into our List View.

```
29   model: ListModel{
30   id: myListModel
31   }
```

For our Model we only need an id, so we have the ability later to interact with it. For the Delegate we will write a bit more.

Delegates are like the housing for our data. The List View takes the data from our Model and puts our Delegate over it, like a mask. This is a performant way of displaying data that does not take up a lot of work. Let us build our Delegate so that we can see how it actually works.

```
32   delegate: MouseArea {
33       id: myDelegate
34   }
```

The delegate property requires a component to work, so we are giving it an item with an id. This id will later be used to make the Delegate interactable.

```
34    width: parent.width
35    height: 50
```

We are going to use the same width and height as our Header. I find that a height of 50 is the perfect height for an item. It has a particularly good readability even on larger displays.

This height is also applicable because of the rise of mobile devices: it is neither too large nor to tiny.

As we want to display text on our Delegate, we also need a Label. So add the Label and give it an id.

```
37    Label{
38    id: titel
39    }
```

The Label inside of a Delegate can get data from the Model using the id of the type of data we want to display in the Label. As an example, you can see here that our text of our Label should be the title text from the data provided by the Model.

This sound oddly complicated, but it allows us to just grab all the data we need for one Item and place the data points.

```
39    text: titelText
```

Next, we need to add the anchors to our Label. The anchors. left will place our Label as far left as the parent's left. We are also adding the achors.verticelCenter. These two create the standard flow of text.

```
40    anchors.left: parent.left
41    anchors.verticalCenter: parent.verticalCenter
```

But we are not finished with this. Currently we only have the title of the task, but I want to also have the data and time of when this task was created. To do that we are going to add another Label to our Delegate. This is going to be our date Label.

```
44    Label{
45    id: date
46    }
```

Give this Label an id, as well as a text property with a reference to the Data Model.

```
44   Label{
45       id: date
46   text: dateText
47   }
```

Here we are also adding the same anchors as before. If we were now to run this app and add some data to our Model, we would not be able to see the Labels, as they overlap each other. This is not really what we want.

```
47   anchors.right: parent.right
48   anchors.verticalCenter: parent.verticalCenter
```

To alleviate the problem, we need to add an anchor.leftMargin. As the name suggests, this adds a margin to our left Anchor, pushing our content to the right. Add this to the title Label.

```
42   anchors.rightMargin: 20
```

We could also add this to our data Label, but a far better solution would be to change the anchor from left to right. This would place our date immediately at the right of our component. But we should also add a margin to the left anchor, so that it is not flush to the end of our window.

When we changed the Label, we are left with this:

Date Label with anchors

```
45   Label{
46   id: date
47   text: dateText
48   anchors.right: parent.right
49   anchors.verticalCenter: parent.verticalCenter
50   anchors.rightMargin: 20
51   }
```

There is still a little bit more we could do that would make the Delegate a little bit prettier, but for now this is not essential. If you have followed along so far, you are left with this:

Finished Delegate with Labels

```
32    delegate: Item {
33        id: myDelegate
34        width: parent.width
35         heigth: 50
36
37        Label{
38            id: titel
39            text: titelText
40            anchors.left: parent.left
41            anchors.verticalCenter: parent.verticalCenter
42                anchors.leftMargin: 20
43        }
44
45        Label{
46            id: date
47            text: dateText
48            anchors.right: parent.right
49            anchors.verticalCenter: parent.verticalCenter
50            anchors.rightMargin: 20
51        }
52    }
```

With this we are finished with the raw version of our Delegate. It works in the way that we can use the Model with the Delegate, and the data should be rendered when we have something in our Model. Next we are going to create the button with which we can input new tasks.

2.4.1.5 Adding Data to the List

This is nearly the most important part of the project, because there is no point in having a List View if we cannot add data to it. So that is what we need to do now.

As already mentioned, we want the add Task button to be in the Footer of our ListView. So let us start by doing this.

Basic Empty Item Footer

```
53     footer: Item {
54       id: footerListView
55     }
```

We start by adding the footer attribute, and to this footer attribute we add an item with a corresponding id.

We also need to add a width and a height to this. As with the header, we are going to set the width to the parent's width, and the height we set to 50.

```
55     width: parent.width
56     height: 50
```

But just an Item wont to what we want, so we will add a round button with a corresponding id. Round buttons are clickable, and that is what we need. Later, we are going to talk a bit more about how buttons work and the best way to set them up and work with them.

For now, you can just use what we have typed out here.

```
53     footer: Item {
54     id: footerListView
55     width: parent.width
56     height: 50
57
58         RoundButton{
59             id: addTaskButton
60         }
61     }
```

The round button should also have a width and a height. For now we are setting these to 40, which is a little bit shorter than the height of our footer. If this does not fit or we want to change it, we can always do this later.

```
58     RoundButton {
59     id: addTaskButton
60     width: 40
61     height: 40
62     }
```

Currently our button would sit in the top left of our footer, and that is not really the way we want it. The best way to get this over to the right is by first giving it a vertical center to the parent's vertical center. Also, we need an anchor to the right.

```
62   anchors.verticalCenter: parent.verticalCenter
63   anchors.right: parent.right
```

We don't want the right anchor here; as with our date Text, we need to position it a little bit to the left so that it is not completely flush to the side of our window.

```
64   anchors.rightMargin: 10
```

It is not possible to jump right into the button click and what it needs to do because we currently have no way of inputting any data. For that purpose, we are going to create a drawer that we can use for inputting data.

Drawers are related to Qt pop-ups, and pop-ups are able to pop up when they are opened. The background is hidden and you can interact with the pop-up, and when you are done then you can click finish and the pop-up closes, and the data is added to the list. That is the way we are going to use it. I find that drawers are better than pop-ups for certain cases. We are also creating this drawer in a separate file and then using it inside of our Main_Page. This is a use for which you will find a lot of reasons. If we were to add all of this to our Main_Page it will be exceptionally long, hard to read, and a real problem if we need to search for one specific thing.

First create a new QML file, which you should know how to do at this point. If you have a problem with it or you do not remember how to do this, go back to the first time we did this or refer to the Git Repository for more help and information. For the name of the QML file we are going with AddTask_Drawer. We have the functionality in front and the type of thing that the file has in it.

If you have done everything as before you should have created this:

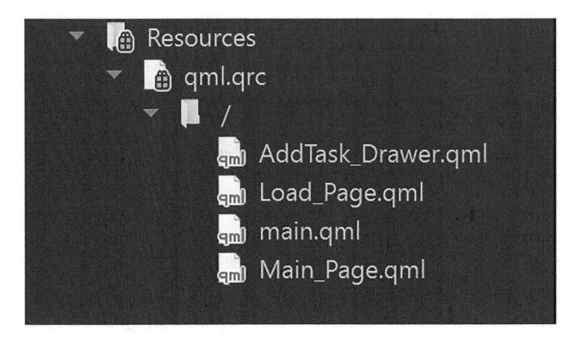

Current Resources at this point

Empty QML file

```
1    import QtQuick 2.0
2
3    Item{
4
5    }
```

As before,. we need to change the import of QtQuick to 2.15 and QtQuick.Controls 2.12, or the newest Version you have available to you. When you have done this, we can jump right into building our Drawer.

First remove the Item Component as well as the Brackets belonging to it. When you have done this, add the Drawer Component to our File.

```
1    import QtQuick 2.15
2    import QtQuick.Controls 2.12
3
4    Drawer {
5
6    }
```

Our Drawer also needs an id. In this case we should use the name of the File as the id, so just put the first letter in lowercase, as ids (the first letter always needs to be lowercase).

```
4   Drawer {
5   id: addTask_Drawer
6   }
```

The width of our drawer should be the width of our window, so use the parent for reference. The height should also be from the parent, divided by 2 so that it only increases by half.

```
5   width: parent.width
6   height: parent.height/2
```

Now that we have a basic drawer, we should make it possible to open it in our Main_Page. This can be done extremely easily in this case. Below our List View component type the name of the file we have our drawer in.

```
69  AddTask_Drawer{
70  id: addTaskDrawer
71  }
```

Now the drawer is usable in our Main_Page, and we are now going to make it possible to open the drawer with the button we created. The click is handled by the onclicked event of our round button.

Basic Round Button with anchors

```
58  RoundButton{
59  id: addTaskButton
60  width: 40
61  height: 40
62  anchors.verticalCenter: parent.verticalCenter
63  anchors.right: parent.right
64  anchors.rightMargin: 10
65  onClicked: {
66
67  }
68  }
```

We can now use the id of our drawer to open it up.

Simple onClicked() event

```
65   onClicked: {
66     addTaskDrawer.open()
67   }
```

This is the only line we need to make our drawer open. As you can see, this is quite easy, and one of the nice things about how ids are used in Qt. You can call any function or method that you want from this id, enabling you to open the drawer up with just one line of code.

If we were to run our application now, we would be greeted by this window. As you can see our header and footer are rendered, and if we were to click on the button in the footer the drawer will open.

Running Task-Master application

The drawer opens from the left of the screen, however. For the type of footer we want it should open from the bottom. Also, the drawer is white, which may not bother you that much, but I find it really distracting and not good to look at. So let's change the background too.

First is the position from where the drawer opens. This can be done through the edge attribute. Go into our AddTask_Drawer file and directly in the drawer, add edge. For our edge we want the drawer opening from the bottom, so we should add Qt.BottomEdge.

```
8    edge: Qt.BottomEdge
```

With this the drawer will be opened from the bottom, and we can drag the drawer up from the bottom. This is a feature that originates from the mobile development aspects of Qt, but if we want to deploy this app on a mobile device this features comes quite in handy.

The background could be done again by using a simple rectangle and placing it inside the drawer, but we are doing it by using the background attributes. Add background as an attribute to our drawer. We also add a rectangle inside it, as the background attribute requires a component to function.

```
9    background: Rectangle{
10
11    }
```

Inside this rectangle we will use anchors.fill: parent to make this rectangle as big as the drawer itself. The color should be the same as the background of the Main_Page. This might seem a bit odd, but because the drawer has a default shadow to it, it will look nice.

```
 9    background: Rectangle{
10    anchors.fill: parent
11    color: "#2C3E50"
12    }
```

We could now also add some round corners or something, but this is a little bit of tinkering and we are going to do this later.

And with that we are finished with the background of our drawer. Now we only need to make the actual input fields that we use to give the user the ability to type in their content.

The input consists of a normal text input we use for our title, and a Date/Time input for our date. This is not that hard, but doing this the right way is not that easy.

```
14    Label{
15    anchors.horizontalCenter: parent.horizontalCenter
16    anchors.top: parent.top
17    anchors.topMargin: 10
18    text: "Add New"
19    color: "white"
20    }
```

First we add a Label. This will be the title of the drawer, and it just says Add New and is cantered horizontally to the parent and at the top of the parent. We position it a little bit below the top of the parent to have a little bit of space between the top and the content. We also give the Label a white text color. This is just to make it a little bit more readable.

Add New

Just below the Label we are now going to add a text field. This will be our way of putting in the data we want.

```
21   TextField {
22     id: titelInput
23     placeholderText: qsTr("Text Field")
24   }
```

Our text field needs an id, so that we can remember and call later, as well as a placeholder text. This placeholder text should always be in your text field; it tells the user what the text field is for and what should be typed into it. We should also change the placeholder text to something more applicable.

```
21   TextField {
22     id: titelInput
23     placeholderText: qsTr("Your Task")
24   }
```

Currently our text field is pinned to the top left, which is not the place we want it to be. To place it in the right place we need three things: a horizontal center to the parent, a top anchor, and a top margin that should be big enough that the Text Field is below our title we created earlier.

```
24   anchors.horizontalCenter: parent.horizontalCenter
25   anchors.top: parent.top
26   anchors.topMargin: 50
```

For the date and time Input we could now create some fancy option with calendar or different filtering options, but that would need a lot of time and greatly increase the complexity of this simple application. First we create an item where the span is below the first text field and has the same with as it.

```
29    Item {
30    width: titelInput.width
31    height: 50
32    anchors.horizontalCenter: parent.horizontalCenter
33    anchors.top: parent.top
34    anchors.topMargin: 125
35    }
```

Inside this item we will have two Text Fields, one for the date and one for time.

Finished date input with placeholder

```
36    TextField{
37    id: dateInput
38    height: parent.height
39    width: parent.width/2.5
40    anchors.left: parent.left
41    placeholderText: "0000-00-00"
42    }
```

Our date input needs an id, as well as a width and a height. The height is the same as the items and the width should be a third of the items. I also added an anchor to the left side, so that it stays on the left. A placeholder text was also added. This is in the expected format which we want, to give the user some sort of guide of how to do it. Next is the time input, which is basically the same text field; the only differences are the id, anchor, and the placeholder text.

Finished time input with placeholder

```
43    TextField{
44    id: timeInput
45    height: parent.height
46    width: parent.width/3
47    anchors.right: parent.right
48    placeholderText: "00:00"
49    }
```

To see what we have done so far, let us run the app. For that click the green arrow in the bottom left that does not have a bug beside it. If you did everything as I have explained here, you will be presented with the app launching.

Task-Master Running Main_Page

If we now click the grey button on the right, the drawer will open and we will see our input form so far.

We could do a lot more with the button, such as changing the color, adding a text, or making an animation.

We are not going to cover animations in this book. This might be a little bit disappointing, but there is not room for it here and most importantly, they are not essential for a beginner. However, in Chapter 3, section 3.2.4, "Qt Animations," I will give you a brief rundown on the animations you can do with Qt, as well as where and how to learn more about them.

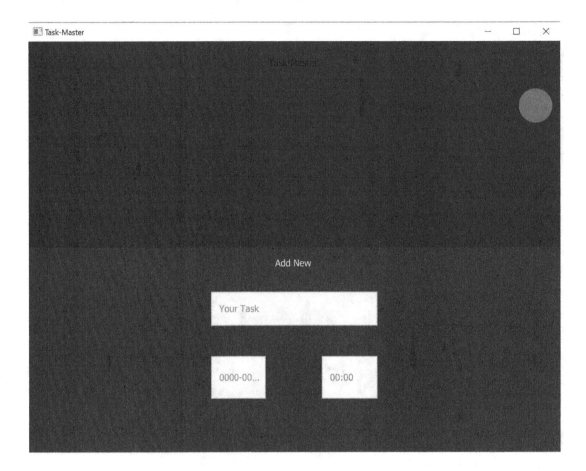

Task-Master Running Add Task Drawer

This looks good so far, and the only thing we need to adjust is the width of our date input. It is currently too short, which leads to our placeholder text being cut off. To change this, go to the date input component and set the width to 2.5 / 3 width of the parent.

```
39   width: parent.width/2.5
```

Now the only thing missing is a button that, when clicked, checks to see if everything was filled out and then creates a new item on our List View.

For our button we are going to use a round button again. This is only for stylistic reasons, because in terms of functionally there is no difference between a normal button or a round button. We are going to center our button horizontally and fix it to the top of our view. The top margin should be about 200, so it is in the right place.

```
51   RoundButton{
52   id: submitButton
53   anchors.horizontalCenter: parent.horizontalCenter
54   anchors.top: parent.top
55   anchors.topMargin: 200
56   text: "Submit"
57   }
```

The button needs to be added below our item. Also, we are going to give the button a width of 200. This would normally not be necessary, as Qt gives the button a procedural with depending on how long the word is. And 200 is a particularly good with for our button.

```
57   width: 200
```

Now we come to our click function. This will be the most important part of our application. So read carefully and refer to the Git Repository when needed.

```
57   onClicked: {
58
60   }
```

First we need to check the inputs we have in our text fields. Normally you would have a lot more tests and checks to see what inputs are performed, but for our purposes we only need to check to see if the inputs are empty or not. If they are not empty, then the program can proceed.

The main part of our application consists of appending a new item to our List Model. This works by using the fieldnames of our data we need and adding the data of our inputs to it. When the button is then clicked, the input is written to the model.

For the dateText we are doing something a little bit more difficult: we are taking the date input and the time input and adding them together, and we are putting " | " in between them as a separator. This takes care of our input. This is the easiest way to add things to our List Model. This could also be used with a for loop to add multiple items at once, so the possibilities are nearly endless with this.

```
58    onClicked: {
59    if(titelInput.text != "" &&
60    dateInput.text != ""&&
61    timeInput.text != ""){
62    myListModel.append({"titelText": titelInput.text,
63    "dateText": dateInput.text + " | " + timeInput.text})
64    }
65    }
```

But if we now would use this to add an item to our List Model, the inputs still retain the data we put in. This is not really what should happen, so we clean the inputs so that they do not retain any data.

```
62    myListModel.append({"titelText": titelInput.text, "dateText":
      dateInput.text + " | " + timeInput.text})
63    titelInput.clear()
64    dateInput.clear()
65    timeInput.clear()
```

We should also close the drawer, because when we put in a new item it should close.

```
67    addTaskDrawer.close()
```

Now let us see what we have done. Save all the files we created and then click the green button below to build and launch our application.

As a side note, I will now explain how a Qt application is actually built (you can skip this if you wish).

Qt compiles an application in three steps. The first is the creation of the .pro file, which describes the application with all modules and how it is structured. Next a makefile is generated and after that, using make, nmake, or jom on Windows, the application is compieled.

This can take a while to compile and then launch. This mainly depends on your machine and how powerful it is. I currently have a fairly powerful machine, but depending on the size of the application it takes up to 30 seconds to compile and build.

I have a Ryzen 9 3950X, with 32 GB of Ram and a GeForce 1080, from Nvidia. It is nowhere near top of the line anymore, but it is more than sufficient for creating applications. I was also able to get Qt Creator running on an old Windows 7 Laptop from 2010, so note that you do not need a lot of power under the hood.

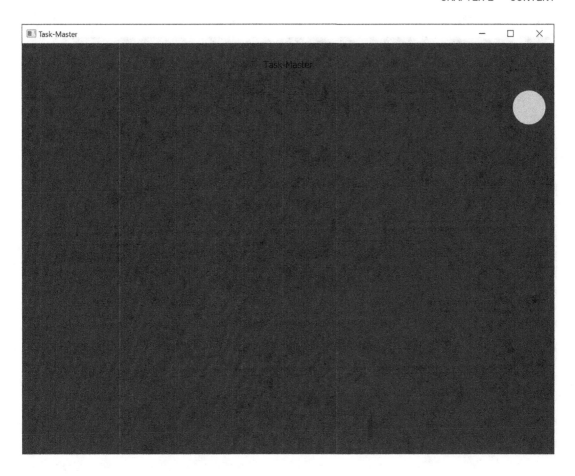

Task-Manager Running Main_Page

When our applications start we will be greeted by our Load_Page, and when our applications have loaded, we are then presented by our Main_Page. Here we have our created List View with our button and our header with our title.

What is shown on screen might not seem like that much, but as always it is not important to have the best visuals but the best functionality, as long as visuals are not your primary goal. We want to learn Qt, so visuals are somewhat important, but the main focus is the functionality.

If we were now to click the button, our drawer opens and we can put our data into the inputs. When we do not put anything into our inputs, clicking the button will not do anything.

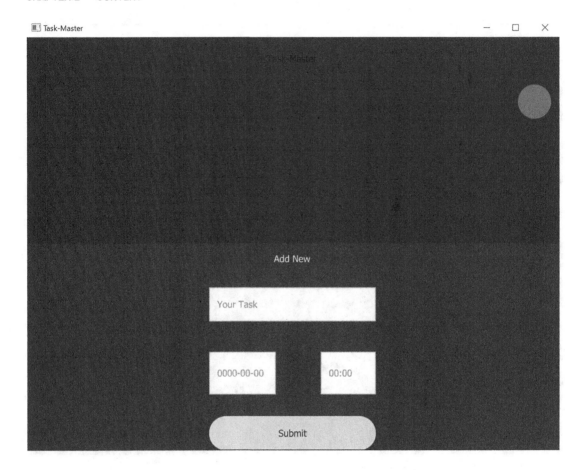

Task-Manger Running Add Task Drawer not filled out

Here you can see the Inputs with corresponding data. Currently we do not have a check function that checks the inputs to see if they are of the current type and have the correct meaning.

We could add this, and you would do so in when creating a real application so that the user is only able to type something in the input you want. But this would be a little bit too complicated for our first application, so we can ignore it for now.

Also, as long as the inputs are not mission-critical, it is not important if the user types in the correct information. When you have a password or email input it might be especially important to check to see if the input is correct, for example, and you do not want SQL-Injections or wrong inputted data.

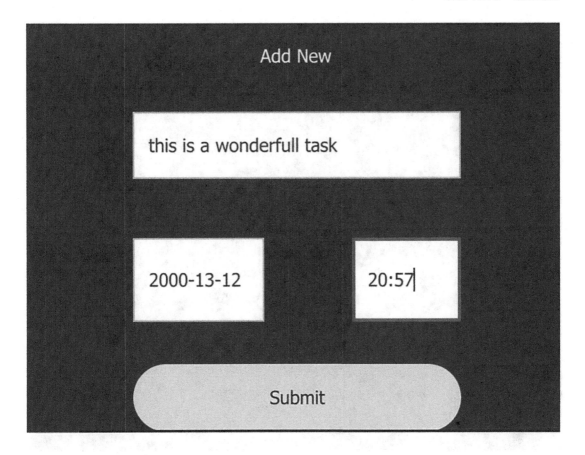

Inputs filled with Data

Here you can see our drawer filled out with data. They are only exemplary data, but as you can see we can put data in because we also had the placeholder text, and most users will tend to also format there input the same way. If they do not format it themselves it is also not a problem, and we could format it later on if we wanted to.

But for our purposes we do not need any formatting as we only are displaying the data, and formatting is not that important at this time. When we now click the Submit button our drawer is closed and a new item is created in our List Model. As you can see here everything is displayed as it should, and we can see all we need.

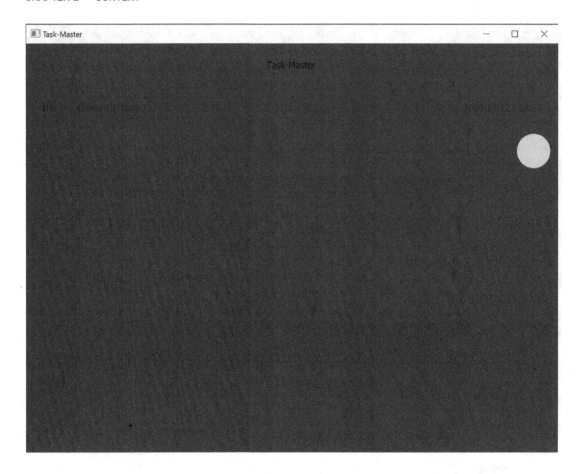

Task-Master newly added Item

Technically we are finished with our application: it has the functionality we want, and it shows what we need it to show. What we are going to do now is make the application a little bit prettier and more usable, and fix up some of the things we skipped over. Although this step is not necessary, I highly recommend it to you because it is one of the things you will do all the time if you are a software developer or engineer.

2.4.1.6 Deleting Data

As we stand right now, we can create new entries in our application. This is all fine and good, but what if you created something you do not want? In that case, you should be able to delete it.

This can be achieved most effectively by a Mouse Area and a onPressAndHold signal. A Mouse Area is a rectangle that is transparent, and you can then interact with that area. You can click it, interact with a mouse with it, drag it, or in this case press and hold it. We can put this inside of our delegate for our ListView and when you press a specific item long enough, it will be deleted from the List Model.

```
32    delegate: Item {
33    id: myDelegate
34    width: parent.width
35    height: 50
36
37    Label{
38    id: titel
39    text: titelText
40    anchors.left: parent.left
41    anchors.verticalCenter: parent.verticalCenter
42    anchors.leftMargin: 20
43    color: "white"
44    }
45
46    Label{
47    id: date
48    text: dateText
49    anchors.right: parent.right
50    anchors.verticalCenter: parent.verticalCenter
51    anchors.rightMargin: 20
52    color: "white"
53    }
54    }
```

The fastest way to do this is by taking our Delegate and changing our item inside it to a Mouse Area. This will make it possible to interact with the delegate automatically, without needing to edit around it.

```
32   delegate: MouseArea {
33   id: myDelegate
34   width: parent.width
35   height: 50
36   onPressAndHold: {
37   listview.currentIndex = index
38   myListModel.remove(listview.currentIndex)
39   }
```

We only need the onPressAndHold signal to make this work. The code needed is not that hard to understand, so let me explain. This signal is activated after 800ms; you could change this with an attribute defined in the Qt Docs, but for our purposes and in general I would always stick to 800ms because it is a timeframe people understand so it is not unexpected, and most people have encountered it already.

```
36   onPressAndHold: {
37   listview.currentIndex = index
38   myListModel.remove(listview.currentIndex)
39   }
```

The first thing we need to do is make the current index of our ListView to the index of the Item we are clicking and holding. After that we take that index and then remove it from our list model. This is the best way to do this without using C++.

With that we are now able to delete items we typed in by simply holding the Item.

2.4.1.7 Cleaning Up the Application

The first thing we can do to make the app a lot prettier is to use another width for our application. Having the right size and composition for your app really heightens the usability.

As we always used anchors for everything, we only need to change the width of our app in one place. What we have in our app is called a responsive layout, so no matter the size of the display the app is usable and works. Changing the width of our application can be done in the main.qml file:

```
4   ApplicationWindow{
5   width: 360
6   height: 720
```

We are going to talk about the different types of resolutions that we can use in a later section, but just remember that there are some universal resolutions such as 1920x1080 or 720x480.

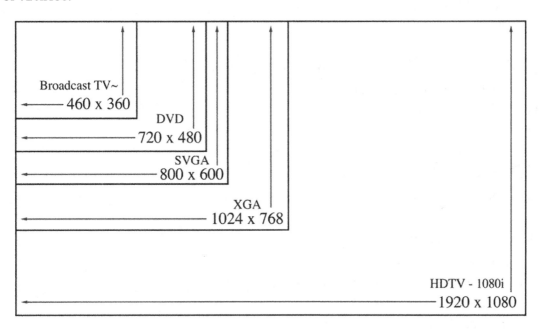

A representation of some common resolutions

This is also the case for mobile applications. Remember that for some smartphones out there the resolution is not 16:9, which means you need to take this into account when you develop for these platforms.

We should also change the color of our text. Having a dark background and black text is not really that readable, so it is best if we change this to a white text color.

Titel of our applciation

```
22    Label{
23    anchors.centerIn: parent
24    text: "Task-Master"
25    color: "white"
26    }
```

Delegate Text for the title of the tasks

```
37    Label{
38     id: titel
39     text: titelText
40     anchors.left: parent.left
41     anchors.verticalCenter: parent.verticalCenter
42     anchors.leftMargin: 20
43     color: "white"
44    }
```

Delegate Text for the date of the tasks

```
46    Label{
47     id: date
48     text: dateText
49     anchors.right: parent.right
50     anchors.verticalCenter: parent.verticalCenter
51     anchors.rightMargin: 20
52     color: "white"
53    }
```

You can also use other colors if you want. The last thing I really want to change is our button that is sued for opening our drawer to put in new items. Currently it is empty and does not display anything. This is not good. If a user were to see this it would not be easy to figure out what the button does. The fastest way to make this a bit more readable is adding a + as the text of the button:

```
60    RoundButton{
61     id: addTaskButton
62     width: 40
63     height: 40
64     anchors.verticalCenter: parent.verticalCenter
65     anchors.right: parent.right
66     anchors.rightMargin: 10
67     text: "+"
```

```
68    onClicked: {
69    addTaskDrawer.open()
70    }
71    }
```

This really improves the readability of the button so that a user can figure out what you mean when they see it.

These are all the changes I would do to finish and make our app a little bit prettier and more usable. You could continue to work and refine the application we have created, but we are moving on to the next topic. Please do not delete the app we have created, as we will be using it as example for other topics later and we are going to implement a few features that are not essential for the application, but are best explained in this type of application.

2.4.1.8 Deploying the Application

Deploying the application is the last topic we are going to review for this application. In this case we are going to deploy it for Windows. If you want to deploy it for another platform, then you can look up the section about that specific platform later in the book.

Now how do you need to go about deploying your application to a MinGW platform? There are a lot of other platforms that you can build and deploy on, but MingGW is what I generally use.

First you need to build your application, which will always create a folder for you in the same directory as your project unless you specified another location. When you have done this, you need to use the Windows search to find the MinGW 8.1 command line interface. If you have opened it up, we can continue.

First we need to go to the directory of our project. You can do this by using the *cd* command and paste the path to the correct directory behind it.

```
 Qt 5.15.2 (MinGW 8.1.0 64-bit)                                    —    □    ×
Setting up environment for Qt usage...

D:\Qt\5.15.2\mingw81_64>cd D:\qtDev\build-cherry-Desktop_Qt_6_0_0_MinGW_64_bit-Debug\debug

D:\qtDev\build-cherry-Desktop_Qt_6_0_0_MinGW_64_bit-Debug\debug>
```

Version here is Qt 5.15.2

Now to the command that gets all our dependencies so that we can actually use the application. If you did not know this already, you cannot use applications built through Qt without also copying the dependencies and the Qt files needed. This is only the case if you did not configure Qt as a static library, but if you have followed along so far you will not have done that.

windeployqt --qmldir [Path to Project] [Path to the .exe File of our Application]

This is the command you need to run the deployment of our application. It is not really difficult to understand. When you located the .exe file that represent our application, you need to type windeployqt. This is the standard tool provided by Qt for deploying applications to the Windows platform. Next, we need to type –qmldir, and behind that we need to specify the path to our project and again the path to the .exe file of our application. It is important that you name the application as well as the .exe at the end to the second path we need for the qmldir.

When you type all this in the CLI you can then press enter and the build process is going to start. This can take a few minutes to up to half an hour depending on the size of the project and how many different dependencies you take with you.

When everything is done, you will see that there are a few new files added to the directory of the .exe. All of these files need to be taken with the .exe file when you want to run this application on another device. The directory right now is also extremely large, between 1 and 3 GB.

This is extremely large for a program, and we are not talking about an overly complicated program; even small ones take this much space to deploy. So keep this in mind.

With this we are done deploying our application to the Windows platform. When you want to learn more about this you can go review the Qt Docs on the matter, and if you are wondering if we are going to do this for Android, we are going to do this in a later section.

2.4.1.9 What We Learned

With this application we learned about List Views in Qt, how to set them up, how to use them, and how we can add items to it. This is not a hard app, but that is not the point. The point was to make you a little bit more comfortable using Qt and figuring out how the structure of a project in Qt works. To give a broad overview, let us have a quick review list of what we have learned:

- List Views

- List Models

- How to add and delete data to a Model

- Buttons

- Text Fields and input types

- How to move through Qt Creator and work with it

The knowledge you learned in this section will be needed later, so feel free to go back and read up on all the topics you want. Most important will be the ListView and the Drawer/ Pop-up component.

These are some of the most important components in Qt, and you cannot really build an application without them. As some people will probably mention you could try building something like a pop-up on your own, and you might be able to do this, but Qt already provides you with a really good solution so I recommend that you use it.

As a side note, Qt also has a lot more components that could really help you in development and make it a lot faster and smother. Also, if there is not a component provided by Qt for a specific instance, then remember that all Qt components can be edited and manipulated through the attributes and properties until they fit your vison and what you need.

Lastly, I am going to give you the full code snippet of our current code. This is mainly for the purpose that if you have come this far, you can always just refer to these screenshots to see how something is done:

main.qml

```
import QtQuick 2.15
import QtQuick.Controls 2.12

ApplicationWindow {
    width: 360
    height: 720
    visible: true
    title: "Task-Master"

    StackView{
        id: contentFrame
        anchors.fill: parent
        initialItem: Qt.resolvedUrl("qrc:/Load_Page.qml")
    }
```

```
    Component.onCompleted: {
        contentFrame.replace("qrc:/Main_Page.qml")
    }
}
```

Load_Page.qml

```
import QtQuick 2.15
import QtQuick.Controls 2.12

Item {
    width: parent.width
    height: parent.height

    Rectangle{
        id: bgRec
        anchors.fill: parent
        color: "#2C3E50"

        BusyIndicator {
            id: busyIndicator
            anchors.centerIn: parent
        }
    }
}
```

Main_Page.qml

```
import QtQuick 2.15
import QtQuick.Controls 2.12

Item {
    width: parent.width
    height: parent.height

    Rectangle{
        id: bgRec
        anchors.fill: parent
        color: "#2C3E50"
    }
```

```
ListView{
    id: listview
    anchors.fill: parent
    header: Item {
        id: headerListView
        width: parent.width
        height: 50

        Label{
            anchors.centerIn: parent
            text: "Task-Master"
            color: "white"
        }
    }
    headerPositioning: ListView.OverlayHeader
    model: ListModel{
        id: myListModel
    }
    delegate: MouseArea {
        id: myDelegate
        width: parent.width
        height: 50
        onPressAndHold: {
            listview.currentIndex = index
            myListModel.remove(listview.currentIndex)
        }

        Label{
            id: titel
            text: titelText
            anchors.left: parent.left
            anchors.verticalCenter: parent.verticalCenter
            anchors.leftMargin: 20
            color: "white"
        }
```

```
            Label{
                id: date
                text: dateText
                anchors.right: parent.right
                anchors.verticalCenter: parent.verticalCenter
                anchors.rightMargin: 20
                color: "white"
            }
        }
        footer: Item {
            id: footerListView
            width: parent.width
            height: 50

            RoundButton{
                id: addTaskButton
                width: 40
                height: 40
                anchors.verticalCenter: parent.verticalCenter
                anchors.right: parent.right
                anchors.rightMargin: 10
                text: "+"
                onClicked: {
                    addTaskDrawer.open()
                }
            }
        }
    }

    AddTask_Drawer{
        id: addTaskDrawer
    }
}
```

AddTask_Drawer.qml

```
import QtQuick 2.15
import QtQuick.Controls 2.12

Drawer {
    id: addTask_Drawer
    width: parent.width
    height: parent.height/2
    edge: Qt.BottomEdge
    background: Rectangle{
        anchors.fill: parent
        color: "#2C3E50"
    }

    Label{
        anchors.horizontalCenter: parent.horizontalCenter
        anchors.top: parent.top
        anchors.topMargin: 10
        text: "Add New"
        color: "white"
    }
    TextField {
        id: titelInput
        placeholderText: qsTr("Your Task")
        anchors.horizontalCenter: parent.horizontalCenter
        anchors.top: parent.top
        anchors.topMargin: 50
    }

    Item {
        width: titelInput.width
        height: 50
        anchors.horizontalCenter: parent.horizontalCenter
        anchors.top: parent.top
        anchors.topMargin: 125
```

```
    TextField{
        id: dateInput
        height: parent.height
        width: parent.width/2.5
        anchors.left: parent.left
        placeholderText: "0000-00-00"
    }
    TextField{
        id: timeInput
        height: parent.height
        width: parent.width/3
        anchors.right: parent.right
        placeholderText: "00:00"
    }
}
RoundButton{
    id: submitButton
    anchors.horizontalCenter: parent.horizontalCenter
    anchors.top: parent.top
    anchors.topMargin: 200
    text: "Submit"
    width: 200
    onClicked: {
        if(titelInput.text !== "" &&
            dateInput.text !== ""&&
            timeInput.text !== ""){
            myListModel.append({"titelText": titelInput.text,
                                "dateText": dateInput.text + " | " +
                                timeInput.text})
            titelInput.clear()
            dateInput.clear()
            timeInput.clear()
            addTaskDrawer.close()
```

```
            }
        }
    }
}
```

This is the only time I will provide you with a code snippet at the end of the project, because the other projects we are going to do are a little too long to really print them out this way. For the other projects you need to go to my Git Hub @BenCoepp. There you will find the project and all the code you are looking for. You can also just search for the project title and Qt or QML behind it. So let us now jump right into the next project.

2.4.2 Hang-Man

This is going to be another extremely easy app to work with. The main principal of how this game works should be familiar with most people in the world: you have a word that the player needs to figure out, the player can select letters from the alphabet, and if the letter is part of the word then it is added at the corresponding place, but if the letter chosen by the player was wrong then the Hang-Man, a figurative stick figure, is going to start becoming visible. When the Hang-Man is visible completely, then the player loses. If the player guesses the word correctly then the player wins.

In essence it is not too complicated, but it allows us to have a look at a few different things we have not looked at so far. First we will learn a bit more with JavaScript and we can also experiment a little bit more with Qt's visual components.

2.4.2.1 Project Creation

First let us create our project. If you are not yet confident with creating projects, remember that you can refer back to the section we did this in previously.

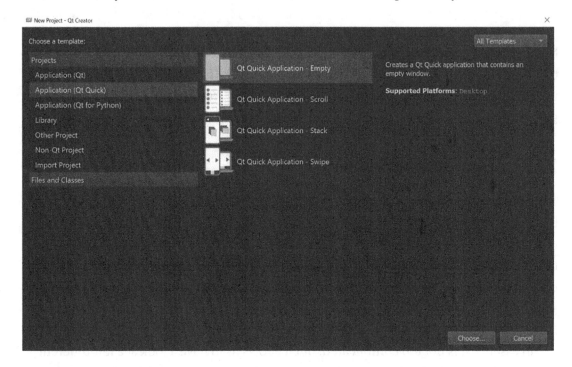

New Project Creation Wizard

As before, we are going to choose Qt Quick Application Empty as our template. We want to make a Qt Quick Application as usual, and I do not like having any boilerplate components inside my application that are going to be thrown out no matter what.

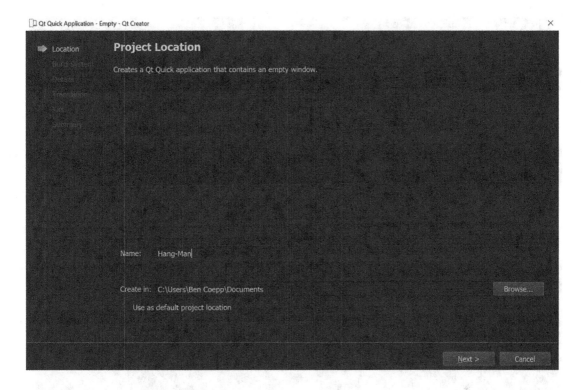

Save location and titel Wizard Page

For the name I chose Hang-Man for our application. For the location you can again choose anything you want, but my recommendation is to choose something that fits the application that you want to build and that you can remember.

The Build System we can leave on qmake, as it is the one Qt has as the default and for us it will do the trick.

I will use 6 for the development of this application. While there is no difference between Qt 6 or 5.15 in terms of what we are building now, you should always use the latest available Qt version, as a lot of bugs and problems will be eliminated.

Again, we do not need a Translation file, so leave this as it is and click next.

For developing the application, we do not need Android for now, so choose MinGW and the appropriate but rate for your system and click next.

Add to version control Wizard page

Here I choose Git as my Version Control. This step is optional, and I will not go over how I am using Git in conjunction with this project, as how Qt interacts and works with Git will be covered in a later section.[26] But having projects like this in your Git Repository is a good thing that I would always recommend.

2.4.2.2 The Load Page and Main Page

Now as before we want to have a simple Load and Main Page setup, so that when the application loads the user is not left wondering what is going on.

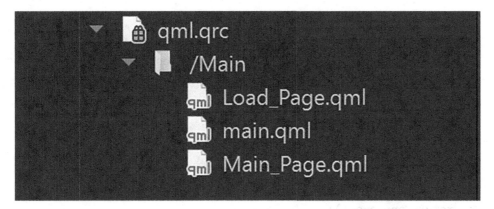

First we need to change the Prefix in which our main.qml file is located, which in this case can be done by right-clicking the Prefix and then selecting change Prefix. Next we need two new files, Load_Page.qml and Main_Page.qml. Both should be located inside our Main Prefix.

If we wanted to run our application now it would spit out a nasty error telling us that this cannot work because our main.qml file does not exist anymore.

```
12:46:05: Starting C:\Users\Ben Coepp\Documents\build-Hang-Man-Desktop_Qt_5_15_2_MinGW_64_bit-
Debug\debug\Hang-Man.exe ...
QQmlApplicationEngine failed to load component
qrc:/main.qml: No such file or directory
QML debugging is enabled. Only use this in a safe environment.
12:46:06: C:\Users\Ben Coepp\Documents\build-Hang-Man-Desktop_Qt_5_15_2_MinGW_64_bit-
Debug\debug\Hang-Man.exe exited with code -1
```

This stems from the fact that we changed the Prefix of our main.qml, so let us jump right over to our main.cpp and fix the problem.

---

[26] In section 3.2.4, "Qt Animation," and in the Rock-Paper-Scissor game project we will be using Git.

```
1    #include <QGuiApplication>
2    #include <QQmlApplicationEngine>
3
4    int main(int argc, char *argv[])
5    {
6        QCoreApplication::setAttribute(Qt::AA_EnableHighDpiScaling);
7
8        QGuiApplication app(argc, argv);
9
10       QQmlApplicationEngine engine;
11       const QUrl url(QStringLiteral("qrc:/Main/main.qml"));
12       QObject::connect(&engine, &QQmlApplicationEngine::objectCreated,
13                       &app, [url](QObject *obj, const QUrl &objUrl) {
14           if (!obj && url == objUrl)
15               QCoreApplication::exit(-1);
16       }, Qt::QueuedConnection);
17       engine.load(url);
18
19       return app.exec();
20   }
21
```

With only the small change in line 11 we are done with the main.cpp file. Now the application starts again, and we want to have the problems again.

```
1    import QtQuick 2.9
2    import QtQuick.Controls 2.5
3
4    Item {
5    width: parent.width
6    height: parent.height
7
8    Rectangle{
9    id: bgRec
10   anchors.fill: parent
11   color: "#2C3E50"
12
```

```
13    BusyIndicator {
14    id: busyIndicator
15    anchors.centerIn: parent
16    }
17    }
18    }
```

Inside of our Load_Page we need this code, which consists out of an item for our root component, a rectangle inside of it for our background, and a Busy Indicator so that we have a visual representation of the loading process. This is not always needed, but it is nice to have because the user wants to know what the app is doing. It is also the entire reason for the Load_Page.

```
1     import QtQuick 2.15
2     import QtQuick.Controls 2.12
3
4     ApplicationWindow {
5     width: 360
6     height: 640
7     visible: true
8     title: "Hang-Man"
9
10    StackView{
11    id: contentFrame
12    anchors.fill: parent
13    initialItem: Qt.resolvedUrl("qrc:/Main/Load_Page.qml")
14    }
15
16    Component.onCompleted: {
17    contentFrame.replace("qrc:/Main/Main_Page.qml")
18    }
19    }
```

Our main.qml file also needs some changes. First we need to update the imports we use inside our main.qml file. Then we can go ahead and change window component to an ApplicationWindow as before, and change the width and height of it to something that more accurately resembles the resolution and aspect ratio of a mobile device. The title we can also change to the title of our application, as this is what we are developing.

Now we can go over the main part of what we need here, our Stack View. This component allows us to load components and replace them when everything is finished loading. We already went over how this works and how to set this up, and both things we changed are the same as what we did in the previous application. If you wanted you could also have copied it over, but then you would not learn anything.

With these things changed we are now done with the Load and Main Page setup; next we are going to go over what the application needs to do and how we want to achieve this.

2.4.2.3 Functionality

We want to make Hang Man, so first we need to clear up what that is and what we need to make it.

The official Wikipedia definition of the game is "a game for two in which one player tries to guess the letters of a word, the other player recording failed attempts by drawing gallows and someone hanging on it, line by line," so it is the one we are using as our guideline for our application. The two players mentioned are for us the computer and the actual player guessing the letters of the word. But what rules do we need for our application?

- Only 10 words allowed for the word the computer chooses, as we do not want to make it too hard for the player.

- The player fails when he chooses 10 letters wrong. When this happens, the Hangman is completed.

These are two rules our application needs to follow to be an interesting game. It is particularly important that you always have rules for your application. This makes it easier to build, as you already have a rough outline of how the application should be worded, what it should feel like, and what it should look like.

To get a little bit more technical, I will also show you now a diagram of how the application works and the interactions the user will perform. I created this diagram using one of the many different websites out there where you can create diagrams for free.

I also recommend that you try building the diagram on the next page on your own.

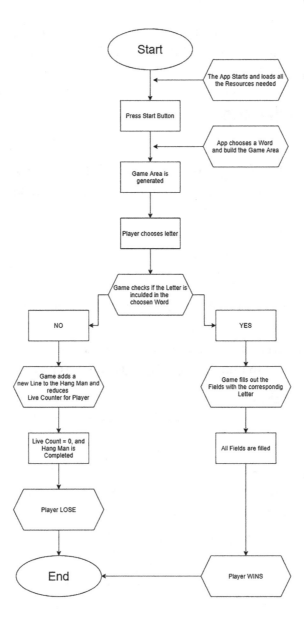

This is a quite simple diagram of how the app should function, but it is all we really need. Why are we doing this here and not for the first application? Diagrams are not always necessary, but here I think it is a good idea to provide one because it allows me to easily explain what we need to do and how to do it, and to demonstrate that I have a clear way of going about building each function we need.

If you are a bit lost then refer to this section and the preceding diagram, which will help you get back on track.

Overall, these diagrams are a must-have for larger and more complex applications and programs and I will go over some of the tricky things you should keep in mind when writing diagrams for Qt applications.

2.4.2.4 Building the App

The first thing we need to build is the game area itself. This is best done by using a Swipe View.[27] It makes it easy for the user to understand how the app works, and we can put all the necessary pages on this Swipe View without needing to create four different files:

Updated imports

```
1    import QtQuick 2.15
2    import QtQuick.Controls 2.12
```

As always, the first thing we need to do is change the imports we currently have in our Main_Page.

After that we can start building our Swipe View. This is the basic boilerplate version of a Swipe View, and you can find the code for it also on the Qt Docs for the Swipe View:

Swipe View in Main_Page.qml

```
 8    SwipeView{
 9    id: swipeView
10    anchors.fill: parent
11    interactive: false
12
13    Item{
14    id: welcomePage
15    width: 360
16    height: 720
17    }
18
19    Item{
20    id: gamePage
21    width: 360
```

---

[27] Read up on section 3.1.3, but Swipe Views are useful because they allow you to have a great UI with swipe functionality, which for a mobile game is great.

```
22    height: 720
23    }
24
25    Item{
26    id: endPage
27    width: 360
28    height: 720
29    }
30    }
31
```

First the Swipe View needs an id and width height. The id is straightforward, and for the width and the height we can use an anchor, so it stays responsive.

We also need the attribute to be interactive, because we do not want the user to swipe and change the view before we want to. So we need to set this to false.

Next we can create three items inside of our Swipe View: the pages we have in our game. Currently they are the same, only the id is different. You can use a property here too, like anchors.fill, which would also work perfectly well here. I just used a fixed size here, as it is easier to understand and because I do not think that it would make any difference in this case. If you were to build this application for production, however, a property would be the better choice.

Next we can create a new file for our Game Page. Currently it would work just sitting inside the Swipe View, but with the amount of things we are going to do inside the Game Page it should really be in its own QML file. So let's create the Game_Page file.

Create the new file the standard way we have done it so far, and a new empty Prefix will be created with the Game_Page.qml file inside of it. We could now use it, but we want to have a more telling Prefix. Next, we should change the Prefix to something a little bit more reasonable.

With this out of the way, we can change the code inside the Game_Page file to the same we have for our Item in our Swipe View. We also need to update the imports to the usual. Now we can import our Game_Page into the place where the game page item is located. But before we can do this, we must import the Prefix into there.

Import Game_Page.qml

```
3    import "qrc:/Game_Page"
```

Importing the Prefix like this allows us to not only use the item in our Game_Page. qml file, but also all the components that are inside this Prefix. When we create a custom button, for instance, we could also use it somewhere else.

Swipe View at this point

```
9    SwipeView{
10   id: swipeView
11   anchors.fill: parent
12   interactive: false
13
14   Item{
15   id: welcomePage
16   width: 360
17   height: 720
18   }
19
20   Game_Page{
21   id: gamePage
22   }
23
24   Item{
25   id: endPage
```

```
26    width: 360
27    height: 720
28    }
29    }
```

Lastly, we need to import the Game_Page as a component and give it an id. With this id we can later interact with the component. It might not be necessary but in my opinion, it is always a good practice to always give every component you are using a telling id.

Now we can start building the Welcome page. One of the first things we should do is give the entire app a background. Currently everything is white, which if you want to go for a clean and Apple-inspired look is great, but I do not like white so let us change it.

```
9     Rectangle{
10    anchors.fill: parent
11    color: "#2c3e50"
12    }
```

Just above our Swipe View we can create a new rectangle with anchors. Fill parent and then set the color to our preferred background color. If you are wondering where I get all these colors from, then you can simply go to my Git Hub or my website and find a color pallet there. You can use that for all the colors I am going to use, or you can use your own colors however you like.

What should be on the actual welcome page? There are only four things that are important:

- The title of the app

- The button to start the app

- Who made the app

- A link to the user agreement and other legal **information**

Why is the last point important? Since I want to publish this application to the Android App Store, to do that the legal documents are required. They are not hard to get and there are a lot of players who can write them for you, but it is very important that you have these when you want to publish an app, because if you do not have them you may face legal liabilities.

Other than that, all the previously mentioned points are fairly straightforward and easy to follow, so let us jump right in.

Welcome Page with titel Label

```
19    Item{
20    id: welcomePage
21    width: 360
22    height: 640
23
24    Label{
25    id: gameTitel
26    anchors.horizontalCenter: parent.horizontalCenter
27    anchors.top: parent.top
28    anchors.topMargin: 50
29    text: "Hang-Man"
30    color: "white"
31    font.pointSize: 50
32    }
```

We can start the build of our Welcome page with the title of our application. I will use a Label for that and position it to the horizontal center and to the top of the parent item. The text is quite self-explanatory, as well as the color. I also choose to give the title a large font size, so that it is clearly visible.

As you are probably aware, we are building the welcome page inside of our Item. This is for two reasons: because this will save us creating another file for it and cluttering up our project tree, and also because I think that it is not such an important page in our application as that it is essential to have it in its own file.

A little side note: the best welcome pages are the ones that are creative and have a unique design. Try to always think of something that best represents the application that you want to build and how this could be best implemented in an application. But do not be afraid to use a standard and safe design when you think this would fit better.

```
34    RoundButton{
35    id: startGameButton
36    anchors.centerIn: parent
37    width: 200
38    height: 200
39    text: "START"
40    font.bold: true
```

```
41    font.pointSize: 38
42    background: Rectangle{
43    anchors.fill: parent
44    radius: 99
45    color: "#fe9000"
46    border.width: 2
47    border.color: "black"
48    }
49    onClicked: {
50    //Logik that Pics a Word
51    }
52    }
```

Next is the round button we will use to start the game. We can center it to the parent give it a size of 200, and the text should be START as we want to start the application when we click this button. We can also manipulate the text a little by making the font bold and the size 38, which is clearly readable but not too large. Now we come to a trickier part. Because we want to have full control over how this button looks and feels we are going to use the background attribute, and we need to do this to use a rectangle as our background. This rectangle should have the same size as the button, and we can also set the color for our button here. I also choose to have a border around the rectangle, which means that now there is a nice black border that clearly separates the button from the background.

Lastly, we can also implement the onclicked signal to the button. We are going to fill this with the necessary logic later, but for now you can know that this will be the place where the application will pick a random word and we will switch to the next page.

```
54    Label{
55    anchors.horizontalCenter: parent.horizontalCenter
56    anchors.bottom: parent.bottom
57    anchors.bottomMargin: 50
58    text: "Made by BEN COEPP"
59    color: "white"
60    font.pointSize: 15
61    }
62
```

```
63    Label{
64    anchors.horizontalCenter: parent.horizontalCenter
65    anchors.bottom: parent.bottom
66    anchors.bottomMargin: 10
67    text: "User Agreement other Legal Stuff"
68    color: "white"
69    font.pointSize: 8
70
71    MouseArea{
72    anchors.fill: parent
73    onClicked: {
74    // Link to Legal Documents
75    }
76    }
77    }
```

We have another two Labels, one that is remarkably like the title Label, just anchored to the bottom and not to the top. The font size is also a little bit thinner than the title Label. The other label is the link to the legal documents. What I usually do is have a label at the bottom of the Page, and inside this Label is a Mouse Area that fills the entire Label. When you click on the Label then you will be bought to another page or to a website where all the legal documents are located.

This is the basic visual information for our welcome page. It is quite simple, and we could also improve on this, for instance by adding animations to the clicking of the button. But for the simplicity of this project, we will not do that.

Next, we should think about the functions needed to start up the game. This means we need a form of model where all the words we want are located inside.

```
14    property var currentWord: ""
15    ListModel{
16    id: wordModel
17    ListElement{
18    word: "TREE"
19    }
```

```
20    ListElement{
21    word: "APPLE"
22    }
23    }
```

For that the only thing we really need to do is create a List Model, give it an id, and place some list elements inside of it. The List Model can be added inside of our Main_Page file, as the data is needed there. You might think of adding this to the Game_Page, but because of inheritance reasons this is not possible, as you would not be able to use the id to call on the data from there.

The only thing we need for data inside of our list elements is the word itself. We could provide more data, such as letter count. But this requires us to always have this data for every list element. It is far easier to generate this data by looking at the word itself each time.

As you can see above the List Model, I also have a property called currentWord, which will be used to hold the word we choose through the function we are building now.

```
60    onClicked: {
61    currentWord = wordModel.get(Math.floor(Math.random() * wordModel.
      count))
62    console.log(currentWord.word)
63    }
```

This function should be placed in our onclicked function for our round button. This generates a random number that is between 0 and the count of the List Model we created.

```
Math.random() * wordModel.count
```

This is what this code does: the function that is around that rounds that number to a full integer, because we are then using this randomly generated integer to get a specific element from our List Model and we cannot use not round integers.

If you were now to run the application and see what currentWord holds on data, you might rely on the fact that we copied the entire model into there. This might not be necessary, but if we were to add more data to each element in our List Model it would be far easier to get that, because we already coded everything to work with the entire object rather than only the data.

If you ask yourself how you get the data from the object, we will have a look at the console.log after our function. Here you can see that you only need to add .word to our currentWord and the object will provide the data for us.

With this we know have a simple function that generates a random word from a list of words we provide. The only thing left to do is to switch the program over to the Game_Page in our application.

```
60   onClicked: {
61   currentWord = wordModel.get(Math.floor(Math.random() * wordModel.count))
62   console.log(currentWord.word)
63   swipeView.setCurrentIndex(1)
64   }
```

Below our console.log you can add this code snippet to make the switch possible. You tell the Swipe View we created earlier to switch to the item that has the index 1, and this is the Game_Page. There are a few more ways you could do this, but I really like this solution as it is remarkably simple and easy to implement.

And with this we are done with the welcome page. Next we are going to create the Game_Page visual components. Mainly we need the following in our app: a ListView that is horizontal that shows all the potential letters that exist and which we filled out; we also need a way to input the letters we want. There are a few ways to do that. You could use a Grid View and display all the letters in the alphabet and then the player could click on them, or we could use a normal text Field and let the player type in the letters. Both variants work, but the latter one is not as refined and good as the first, and we would also need to implement a check function so that the player only types in letters that are allowed. We will be using a Grid View for that.

We also need a way to display the Hang Man in such a way so that when the count of the players wrongly-guessed letters increases, the image is made more and more visible.

But first let us start by creating the input fields for our application.

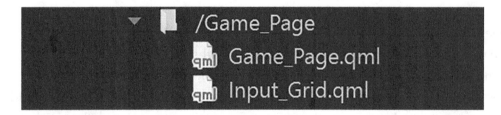

First we need to create a new file under our Game_Page Prefix. For the sake of consistency, we should call it Input_Grid.

```
4    GridView {
5    id: inputGrid
6    width: parent.width
7    height: parent.height/3
8    anchors.bottom: parent.bottom
```

The Grid View we create is similar to the type of List Views we did so far. We first need an id, as well as a width and height. Both can be derived from the parent. We also can immediately set the anchors to the bottom of our parent's bottom, as we know that that is where we want to locate our Grid View.

```
9    cellHeight: 50
10   cellWidth: 50
```

These are two new attributes we did not yet discuss. The size of each item inside the Grid is normally 100, but that is far too large for our needs. We can set this to 50.

```
11   model: ListModel{
12   ListElement{
13   letter: "A"
14   }
15   ListElement{
16   letter: "B"
17   }
```

The List Model is a real bummer because we need to create a new list element for each letter in the alphabet. We could also do this programmatically, but from what I know there are only a few ways to do this that make the process a little bit easier then typing everything out, so I leave this decision to you.

```
91   delegate: MouseArea{
92   width: 50
93   height: width
94   onClicked: {
95   borderRec.border.width = 1
```

```
96    //Send letter to test function
97    }
98
99    Rectangle{
100       id: borderRec
101       anchors.fill: parent
102       color: "transparent"
103       border.width: 0
104       border.color: "white"
105
106       Label{
107       anchors.centerIn: parent
108       text: letter
109       font.pointSize: 10
110       font.bold: true
111       color: "white"
112       }
113       }
114    }
```

Now we come to the delegate of our Grid View. As with the List View we had before, this can be seen as a mask for all our data. It consists of a Mouse Area that is the same size as the cell size we created earlier. Inside this Mouse Area we have a rectangle, which is transparent color-wise but has a border, which is white but has a width of 0, which will be important later. Inside this rectangle will be a Label, which has as its text attribute the letter data from our List Model. With this our delegate displays the data.

I also added the onclicked event to our Mouse Area, and we will later add the link to the check function later. But for ease of displaying which letter has already been clicked, I added to line 96 that when you click a letter a white border forms around it. This means you always know what you clicked.

```
1    import QtQuick 2.9
2    import QtQuick.Controls 2.5
3
```

```
4    Item{
5    id: gamePage
6    width: 360
7    height: 640
8
9    Input_Grid{
10   id: inputGrid
11   }
12   }
```

Now we can go over to the Game_Page.qml file and add our Input_Grid as a component. We also should give it an id. The grid will be displayed inside our application and we can click the letters.

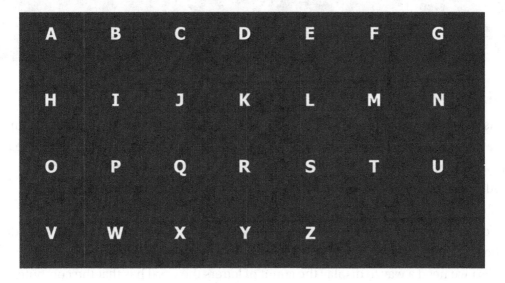

Input Grid View

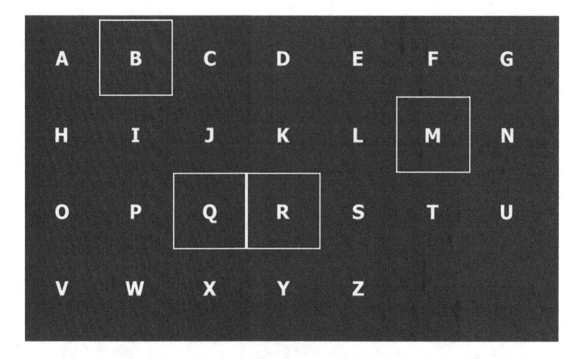

Input Grid with selected letters

As you can see, all is working as intended. You might be wondering about the empty space in the bottom left. This will be a retry option. I know it makes the game really easy, but for developing the game an easy mode is really hand, so I will implement one.

Also, this button could later be used to start a new round of Hang Man if you are not able to guess the word, or if you do not like it. This is a stylistic and functional unnecessary option I want to implement, but sometimes you need to think a lot out of the box and sometimes you need to make room for these stylistic choices.

Next we need a way to display the count of letters the word has that the computer randomly provided us. So let's implement that.

```
14    property var currentWord: ""
15    property var wordCount: 0
16    ListModel{
17    id: listModelCount
18    }
```

First we need to add another property to our Main_Page.qml file. We should call it wordcount; a better name would be letter count, but that will be used later on. The property should be initialized with 0. Below that we need to create a List Model, with an id. This model does not need any elements built in so leave it as it is.

```
9    ListView{
10     id: listViewLetterCount
11     width: parent.width
12     height: 50
13     orientation: ListView.Horizontal
14     anchors.bottom: parent.bottom
15     anchors.bottomMargin: inputGrid.height+20
16     interactive: false
17     model: listModelCount
18     delegate: MouseArea{
19     width: 50
20     height: parent.width/10
21
22     Rectangle{
23     anchors.bottom: parent.bottom
24     anchors.horizontalCenter: parent.horizontalCenter
25     width: parent.width-10
26     height: 4
27     color: "white"
28     }
29     }
30     }
```

As already mentioned, we are going to use a List View as our display of how many letters are needed. The List View in itself is remarkably similar to what we are already used to seeing. The model used is the one we created earlier; the binding throws the id in this case even through the project structure.

To place the List View above the Input Grid, we make an anchor.bottom and then a bottom margin that has as its value the height of the Input Grid + 20. This means it is right above the inputs but not too far above.

We also made the ListView not interactive, because we do not wont the player scrolling around and doing things they should not do. This is the best way to prevent this.

A new attribute we used here is the orientation of the ListView. This turns the ListView on its side and displays all the items horizontally. If you want to do something similar it is a good idea to do it this way.

The delegate we created is really simple. It is a basic Mouse Area without any click functionality and a rectangle at the bottom of this Mouse Area that is a little bit smaller than the width of the Mouse Area. This will be the spaces that tell the player how many letters the word has.

```
64    onClicked: {
65    currentWord = wordModel.get(Math.floor(Math.random() * wordModel.count))
66    wordCount = currentWord.word.length
67    for(var i = 1; i <= wordCount; i++){
68    listModelCount.append({"space": "-"})
69    }
70    console.log(currentWord.word)
71    swipeView.setCurrentIndex(1)
72    }
```

And here is the magic that creates these lines. Basically, we insert into the onclicked event that we used some new code. First we need to get the length of the word we randomly generated. For that we can simply call currentWord, get the word from the object, and then get the length from it.

With the length we can then create a for loop that ges from 1 to the length of the generated word and for each adds a new item to the List Model for listModelCount. The data we add is not important, so add whatever you want. We just need the number of items as letters in our word.

When you start up our application you can see that for the word Apple the correct number of spaces was created. These spaces will always form from left to right or the other way around. They will never generate from the middle. Therefore, everything we do needs to be aligned to this.

I do not really like this, as it does not look as good as I want to have it. But it does the job and the perspective it creates is really good.

Now we need to have a look at the check function that checks to see if the letter pressed is in the word and if so, places the word at the appropriate index inside a new ListView we need to create later on.

But first let us start with the check function.

```
94   onClicked: {
95   borderRec.border.width = 1
96   //Check if letter is included in the Word
97   if(currentWord.word.match(letter)){
98   console.log("Yes Letter:" + letter + " is in the Word")
99   }else{
100  //Player did not find letter
101  console.log("NO Letter:" + letter + " is in the Word")
102  }
103  }
```

With this quite simple if statement we can now first check to see if the letter is included, and we then give a console log that it was included.

If you did everything until now and you were to start up the application you might rely on that working for the first letter in the word, but for all the other letters it will not. This is because we are not searching for the letter but for the exact matching one. So upper- and lowercase matter. We could now set a parameter to the match function and disable the problem, but because I want to have all the word in bold and uppercase anyway, we can change them in our word List Model.

```
19   ListModel{
20   id: wordModel
21   ListElement{
22   word: "TREE"
23   }
```

```
24    ListElement{
25    word: "APPLE"
26    }
27    }
```

Now you might rely on that we are not done with the functions we need, so let us finish them.

World List View

```
32    ListView{
33    id: listViewWord
34    width: parent.width
35    height: 50
36    orientation: ListView.Horizontal
37    anchors.bottom: parent.bottom
38    anchors.bottomMargin: inputGrid.height+40
39    interactive: false
40    model: ListModel{
41    id: wordOutputModel
42    }
43
44    delegate: MouseArea{
45    width: 50
46    height: parent.width/10
47
48    Label{
49    anchors.centerIn: parent
50    font.pointSize: 20
51    font.bold: true
52    color: "white"
53    text: letter
54    }
55    }
56    }
```

First we need another horizontal ListView just like the one we built for the spaces. The delegate is only different in that it does not have a rectangle inside it, but instead a Label that gets the letter from the model.

This is for all intents and purposes a normal List View. If you compared it to the one we created in our first application, the only difference is the orientation.

```
94    onClicked: {
95    borderRec.border.width = 1
96    //Check if letter is included in the Word
97    if(currentWord.word.match(letter)){
98    // Found Letter
99    console.log("Yes Letter:" + letter + " is in the Word")
100   var index = currentWord.word.indexOf(letter)
101   console.log(index)
102   wordOutputModel.insert(index, {"letter": letter})
103   }else{
104   //Player did not find letter
105   console.log("NO Letter:" + letter + " is in the Word")
106   hangManCounter++
107   buildHangMan()
108   }
109   winCheck()
110   }
```

The primary function that handles everything is only really changed in that aspect in that we create a var called index and then found the index of the letter that was selected. This is only the case when the letter matches the current word.

Also, when the word does not match a counter is increased.

```
14    property var hangManCounter: 0
15    property var currentWord: ""
16    property var wordCount: 0
```

This counter should be added to the Main_Page.qml file above the other properties. This counter is especially important later when we come to the winCheck function.

winCheck function at this point

```
127    function winCheck(){
128    if(wordOutputModel.count == wordCount){
129    //Player has won
130    console.log("Player won")
131    }else if(hangManCounter == 10){
132    //Hang-Man is complete
133    console.log("Player lost")
134    }
135    }
```

The winCheck function in its simplicity checks to see first if the count of added words is equal to the wordcount we generated earlier. This would mean for the program that all letters were found and the player has won: a quite simple check. When the player loses, the check is really not different. Thanks to the counter we implemented earlier we can just check to see if the counter is equal to 10. If that is the case, then the player has lost.

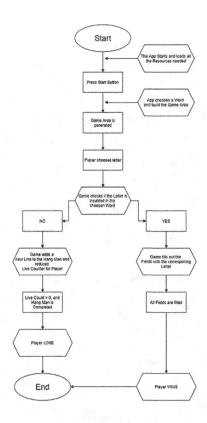

Currently we are at this point in developing our application, as highlighted in the diagram. As you can see we have already finished quite a lot in our development, but there are still a lot of things we need to complete and finalize.

This will probably take a while, but always refer back to our section about the functionality of our application where you can check how far you have come and what you have achieved.

If we were to start the application now and begin playing, you would see two things happening.

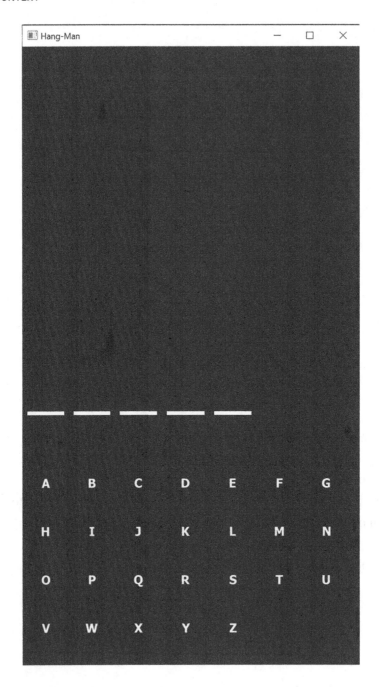

Running Hang-Man Application

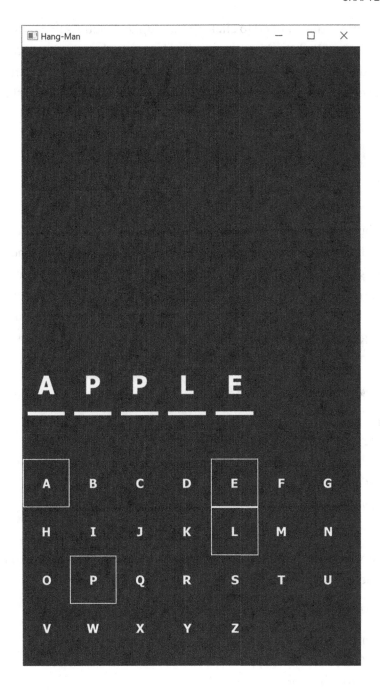

Running Hang-Man Application Word filled out

The game works, but you need to click on the duplicate letters two times so that the appropriate fields are filled. And you must select letters in the way the word is formed. So here the word was Apple. If you did not start with A and worked your way down from there, you will get an error telling you that there is no forth index in the List Model, which is true.

```
qml: 4
qrc:/Game_Page/Game_Page.qml:40:16: QML ListModel: insert: index 4 out of range
```

Console Output

These two bugs must be fixed so that the application works as it should.

Other than that, you can see that the application works as intended and even better than you might suspect. The win is correctly accepted, and we can go from there.

For the sake of clarity I will first finish the game so that it is playable completely, and then we will review the two bugs. They are not game-breaking, and they can be fixed.

First we are going to build a Hang Man out of rectangles. After that we are going to import the file and build a function that makes the parts visible depending on the counter.

Console.log that prints out when word is found

```
103    }else{
104    //Player did not find letter
105    console.log("NO Letter:" + letter + " is in the Word")
106    hangManCounter++
107    buildHangMan()
108    }
```

Right below where we count up the counter for the Hang Man, we need to add the name of the function we need to build.

if clause for making the Hang-Man visible based on the hangManCounter

```
138    function buildHangMan(){
139    if(hangManCounter == 1){
140    rec1.visible = true
141    }else if(hangManCounter == 2){
142    rec2.visible = true
143    }else if(hangManCounter == 3){
144    rec3.visible = true
```

```
145   }else if(hangManCounter == 4){
146   rec4.visible = true
147   }else if(hangManCounter == 5){
148   rec5.visible = true
149   }else if(hangManCounter == 6){
150   rec6.visible = true
151   }else if(hangManCounter == 7){
152   rec7.visible = true
153   }else if(hangManCounter == 8){
154   rec8.visible = true
155   }else if(hangManCounter == 9){
156   rec9.visible = true
157   }else if(hangManCounter == 10){
158   rec10.visible = true
159   }
160   }
```

The function itself is not that complicated, as you can see it is just a big if statement that filters the current state of the counter out and then tells the corresponding rectangle to turn visible. It is nothing special, and there are a few better ways to do this. One would be to use a switch case, but you cannot really make this any smaller, unless you want to make it a bit more complicated.

```
MouseArea {
        id: root
        anchors.top: parent.top
        anchors.horizontalCenter: parent.horizontalCenter
        width: 360
        height: 360

        Rectangle {
            id: rec1
            x: 19
            y: 319
            width: 87
            height: 20
```

```
        color: recColor
        visible: false
    }

    Rectangle {
        id: rec2
        x: 52
        y: 38
        width: 20
        height: 283
        color: recColor
        visible: false
    }

    Rectangle {
        id: rec3
        x: 52
        y: 38
        width: 189
        height: 20
        color: recColor
        visible: false
    }

    Rectangle {
        id: rec4
        x: 221
        y: 39
        width: 20
        height: 54
        color: recColor
        visible: false
    }
```

```
Rectangle {
    id: rec5
    x: 189
    y: 89
    width: 84
    height: 84
    color: "transparent"
    radius: 99
    border.width: 15
    border.color: recColor
    visible: false
}

Rectangle {
    id: rec6
    x: 221
    y: 168
    width: 20
    height: 91
    color: recColor
    visible: false
}

Rectangle {
    id: rec7
    x: 200
    y: 231
    width: 20
    height: 91
    color: recColor
    rotation: 210
    visible: false
}
```

```
Rectangle {
    id: rec8
    x: 242
    y: 231
    width: 20
    height: 91
    color: recColor
    rotation: 150
    visible: false
}

Rectangle {
    id: rec9
    x: 252
    y: 170
    width: 20
    height: 91
    color: recColor
    rotation: 130
    visible: false
}

Rectangle {
    id: rec10
    x: 190
    y: 170
    width: 20
    height: 91
    color: recColor
    rotation: 230
    visible: false
}
}
```

Here I have the Hang Man in its parts as code snippet for you. As I did it here is not recommended; it is not responsive, and it could break very easily. But if you wanted to make this responsive then good luck. This would be complicated and it would take a long time. A far easier solution is to leave the size of the Mouse Area at a fixed angel, and just make it so that it is anchored to the correct position at the top. This means that if you were to use this app on a larger screen then you would only see the Hang Man as tiny. But that is an unavoidable sacrifice that you need to make from time to time.

Mouse Area fixed Version

```
9    MouseArea {
10   id: root
11   anchors.top: parent.top
12   anchors.horizontalCenter: parent.horizontalCenter
13   width: 360
14   height: 360
```

Just by changing the Mouse Area like this you can nearly completely eliminate the problem, and we now have a working Hang Man.

As I already mentioned, this is a really bad way of doing the Hang-Man. It is not responsive and it can break very easily when we are not careful, and from a software engineering standpoint it is very ugly. A far better solution would be to have multiple images and then cycle through these images using a simple function. It is still not great, but a lot prettier as a bunch of rectangles.

Another solution would be to use multiple SVG images, and then color them in depending on if they need to be active or not. It would mean that you need several of these images, but it is also a bit nicer.

But all of these options are very time- and resource-intensive and for the simple act of learning, they are not necessary. If you want to you can try to improve this on your own when you are done with the project.

Here you have an example where the Hang Man is completed. Another thing we can do to improve the overall game is to change the colors of the rectangles for the Hang Man into something a little bit more colorful. The main thing I want to emphasize here is not repetitive teaching, but how to make it easier to change something like this later.

Currently all the colors we used are on every component, meaning that if you were not to change this color you would need to change this on every rectangle. Right now this is unavoidable, but in the future we can do something a little bit better.

New added property recColor

```
4    Item{
5    id: gamePage
6    width: 360
7    height: 640
8
9    property var recColor: "#fe9000"
10
11   MouseArea {
12   id: root
```

First add a property right below our item. It is not possible to place it inside of our Mouse Area, as there it would not work. We can call it recColor, as it holds our color. This color can be found in the color pallet for this project, on my website, or the Git Repository for this project. Now we can copy and paste the name of the property in place of an actual color. This means that when you want to change the color now you can just change it here and not at every place. This can also be used in larger projects where you have even more places where color is important.

Now it looks better, and the only things remaining is the win or loss page.

The way we can do it is by changing the currently index of our Swipe View in our Main_Page to that of the last item in the Swipe View.

```
106    Item{
107    id: endPage
108    width: 360
109    height: 640
110
111    Label{
112    anchors.top: parent.top
113    anchors.topMargin: 50
114    anchors.horizontalCenter: parent.horizontalCenter
115    text: "PLAYER"
116    font.pointSize: 50
117    font.bold: true
118    color: "white"
119    }
```

The last page starts off simple with just a Label that says PLAYER. We position the Label at the top of our view and center it horizontally. We also give it a large size and make it bold. The color of the rectangle should also be white.

```
121    Label{
122    id: winLossLabel
123    anchors.top: parent.top
124    anchors.topMargin: 150
125    anchors.horizontalCenter: parent.horizontalCenter
126    text: ""
127    font.pointSize: 50
128    font.bold: true
129    color: "#fe9000"
130    }
131
132    Label{
133    anchors.bottom: parent.bottom
134    anchors.bottomMargin: 150
135    anchors.horizontalCenter: parent.horizontalCenter
136    text: "WANT TO"
137    font.pointSize: 30
```

```
138    font.bold: true
139    color: "white"
140    }
```

Next we have another Label. It is similarly positioned and styled as the first one, but a bit larger. Also, the color is the orange we have used so far. The text attribute is currently empty and is filled with the win or loss function we created earlier.

```
128    function winCheck(){
129    if(wordOutputModel.count == wordCount){
130    //Player has won
131    console.log("Player won")
132    winLossLabel.text = "WON"
133    }else if(hangManCounter == 10){
134   //Hang-Man is complete
135    console.log("Player lost")
136    swipeView.setCurrentIndex(2)
137    winLossLabel.text = "LOST"
138    winLossLabel.color = "#d23742"
139    }
140    }
```

As you can see, we were able to use the id we gave the Label to change what it says and what color it is by calling the id, and then changing the attribute. Depending on whether the player wins or loses we want to display that as text, and if the player loses then we want a different color than is normally the case.

The other Label is amazingly simple, and just anchored to the bottom.

```
142    Label{
143    anchors.bottom: parent.bottom
144    anchors.bottomMargin: 100
145    anchors.horizontalCenter: parent.horizontalCenter
146    text: "TRY"
147    font.pointSize: 20
148    font.bold: true
149    color: "#fe9000"
150    }
```

This one is more or less the same, only smaller and with a different color then the first:

Return Button

```
152    RoundButton{
153    anchors.bottom: parent.bottom
154    anchors.bottomMargin: 50
155    anchors.horizontalCenter: parent.horizontalCenter
156    width: 200
157    height: 40
158    text: "AGAIN"
159    font.bold: true
160    font.pointSize: 30
161    background: Rectangle{
162    anchors.fill: parent
163    radius: 99
164    color: "#fe9000"
165    }
166    onClicked: {
167    swipeView.setCurrentIndex(0)
168    }
169    }
```

And lastly we have the button with which you can go back to the first page: a quite simple button quite like the button we created to start the game. For the onclicked function, it is a one liner, with which you jump back to the first page.

Just jumping back to the first page is not going to work, because if you were to begin a new game, all the data from the game before would still be in the models. So we need to clear the models of any data. You might think of doing this here were we changed to the first page, but that would not work. The best way to do it is by doing it immediately in the winCheck function.

WinCheck Function

```
128    function winCheck(){
129    if(wordOutputModel.count == wordCount){
130    //Player has won
131    console.log("Player won")
```

```
132    swipeView.setCurrentIndex(2)
133    winLossLabel.text = "WON"
134    wordOutputModel.clear()
135    listModelCount.clear()
136    }else if(hangManCounter == 10){
137    //Hang-Man is complete
138    console.log("Player lost")
139    swipeView.setCurrentIndex(2)
140    winLossLabel.text = "LOST"
141    winLossLabel.color = "#d23742"
142    wordOutputModel.clear()
143    listModelCount.clear()
144        }
145    }
```

With the two models cleared, the game can begin anew.

Now with the app built, let us have a look at what we built to see how everything looks. This is just a recap of what we have done in this project and I will not be able to provide all the images of every component, as this would be far over 100 pages. If you want the code then go to my website bencoepp.io or my Git Hub BenCoepp, where you can find nearly everything you are looking for when it comes to the code for this project.

As you can see, the application is working as intended and does what we want. The game loop also works. And with this we are done with the application. In this project you learned something about:

- Horizontal List Views

- Model structuring

- Larger projects

- Creating custom components

- Interconnecting components

- Functioning game loops

These might not seem that important, and this was not a large or complicated project. But that was not the intention when I created it: it was for the simple learning experience you can gain from creating a small game or application on your own.

And on a side note, repetition is key in my opinion for learning something like a new framework or programming language. You cannot learn something effective when you do not repeat it over a dozen times. So maybe you should reread the book from time to time when you want to practice a little.

2.4.2.5 Deploying the Application

Now to the actual deploying of our application. This is a particularly important part of most developments and projects. But unfortunately, it is not covered very often.

Because we want to deploy our application for Android, you need to have followed the steps in the early sections where we set up the Android SDKs and NDKs we need for this.

Now to the actual deployment of our application to an Android device. First you need to go to the Projects tab at the left side. When you click on it, it will reveal a list of all the available packages you currently have installed, and those that can be used on the project will have a little green plus beside the Icon.

The first thing is to add all the Android Qt Kits. There are four different kind of kits; in some existing versions they were bundled up into one kit, but here you need to add all four.

The next thing is to click in on one of these kits, which will open up the Build Settings for the specific kit. Here you can manipulate and edit a lot of the underlying setting of how Qt build Android packages. If you want to learn more about all the settings that exist here and that should you manipulate, you can read about that in the Qt Docs.

I usually enable all the kits I tend to use right from the get-go. I know that we did not do this in this project, mainly because I did not want to confuse you. But if you are going to create your own projects from now on, you can also active and configure all the kits you are going to use.

Build Android APK Drop-Down

The first thing we need to do here is to open the Build Android APK. When you open that you see the content depicted in the preceding screenshot.

Signed signature added to our Build Android APK settings

The first thing we need to do here is sign our application. If you have never deployed or published an application, you might wonder why we need this and what it is used for. In professional development, especially when you want to publish an application on the App Store or Play Store, we need to have a keystore. This authenticates the application to you so that nobody can steal your application and publish it, because for that they would need this keystore.

So if you have one, then click browse and find your keystore, but if you do not have one, then click on create and let us create one.

Create keystore Wizard

This will open up a pop-up that will ask us for a lot of information. Everything should be self-explanatory. Remember that you will need to remember the password. You cannot change the password if you forgot it, so remember it or you will not be able to publish your applications anymore.

Also, the information about your distinguished names is important for Google or Apple, so do not lie here or you can get in a lot of trouble.

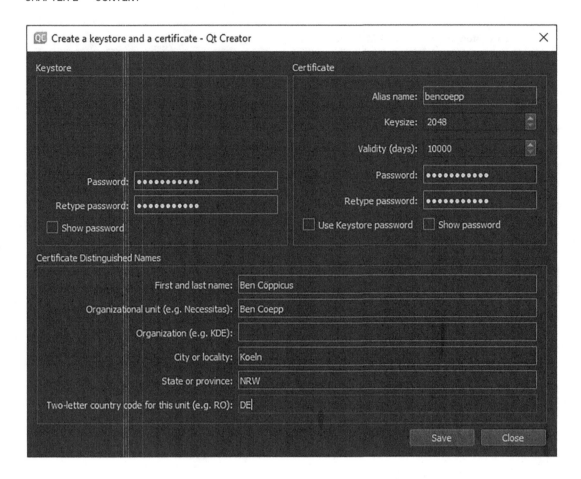

Filled out Create keystore Wizard

When you have filled everything out, check the inputs, as there is no editing or reducing this, and then you click save. This will then ask you for a location where the keystore should be saved. Here you should heed my words carefully. It is particularly important that this keystore is never deleted. Save it multiple times, on different devices, and in the cloud if you can. If you lose the keystore you are not able to publish this application anymore.

Enter keystore Password Pop-up

If you then clicked Save, it will create the keystore and save it in the destination you selected. Next it will close the first pop-up and open a new one right away. Here it will ask for the password of the keystore you just created.

If you still remembered what you had as your password, type it in and click OK.

Create Template button

The next thing we need to do is create a new Android template. If you have never created an Android application this will seem pointless and a little bit confusing, but it is necessary, so create it.

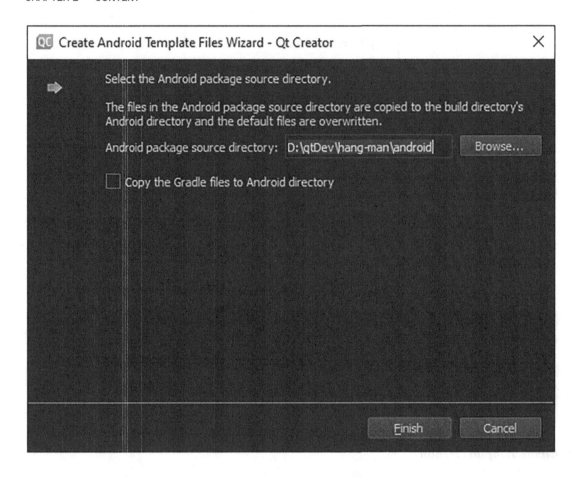

First it will open a wizard, where it asks you where the Android package source should be. You can leave everything as it is; there is no real point in changing the source of the Android files, as this just creates a lot of problems down the line. Also do not select the checkbox, as this is something that does not work for our project here, so leave it as it is.

Android Template Files in the Project Structure

When you clicked finish, a few new file scans can be found in our project directory. These are the files we created just now by creating a new template.

Some of these files are less important than others, but the most important file is the AndroidManifest.xml, which is a file that holds all the information about our application.

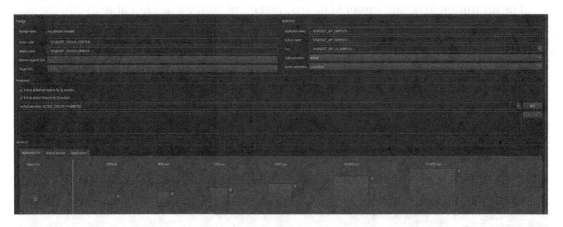

As you can see there are many things we can fill out here. Typically, you will tend to do this only once when you create the file the first time, and then only occasionally change a few things in here when you really need to. Other than that you will leave this file as it is.

The first patch of important information is for the package. Here you can find the package name, the version code, and name as well as the minimum and target SDK. For you this is properly empty or filled with some random items, so let us fill it with something a bit more fitting.

The package name should always be comprised of two things: the name of the application and the name of yourself or your company. In my case it was hangman. bencoepp. hangman, because this is the application's name and bencoepp because that is the alias I usually use.

Next is the version code and name. For now I just leave it as it is, mainly because I currently do not need it, and you will only change this if you release this software.

The minimum SDK and target SDK are greyed out, and we are not able to edit them. In most cases you probably can leave this as the Qt default. The only reason you might want to change this is because you have an application that is run by people that do not have the newest device and you require an old SDK version. But other than that, leave it as it is.

Right next to the package information is the information about the application. These settings are even easier to understand.

The Application Name, Activity Name, and Run are always configured with the Application Name, and for us in this case it is Hang-Man. These three inputs serve the same purpose of being the display name, as well as the name Android shows when you run the app.

Next, we have the style extraction property. This is a new setting that you can use when you want to differentiate the different rendering and styling options Android has. For instance, if you want to use Android's Native styling that you can find on your Android Device, you would select Default. Because we made all or styling on our own, we can choose none here.

Lastly, we have the screen orientation, which tells Android how the application is orientated. You have the typical assortment of Portrait, Horizontal, Landscape, and a few more. For us Portrait is the most sensible one, so we need to select that.

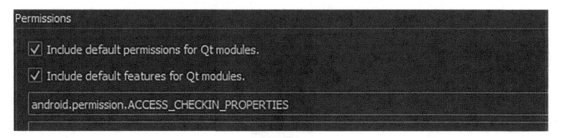

Android Manifest Permissions

Just below the package and application information, we have the permissions. Android is difficult in terms of what applications are allowed to do. Because Qt requires a few default permissions, leave the checkboxes as well as the line below them as they are; you cannot really do anything about the permissions needed, so basically you can nearly always have this as Qt has it as default.

Now we can come to the advanced options. These are interesting options that really help you with a lot of things, such as setting an application icon for your application. If someone downloads your application you have the application icon as your icon of your application. This icon also shows when you run the application.

Next, we have the Splash Screen. This is also a new feature that allows us to set a Splash Screen for the application. While the application loads, you will have this Image on display.

Before that you had the option of building an extremely complicated loading setup that handles this, or you just did not have a Splash Screen. Because I did not create a Splash Screen, I just set the application icon as the image.

Now that we have edited all the settings, we need to deploy our application. Before we can do this, we need to do a few things.

First you need to plug your Android device into your PC with a USB Cable. If you have done that, you can click on the green arrow just as we did before when we wanted to launch our application.

If you have problems doing the next few things, you might want to read ahead to section 2.4.3.10, "Deploying the Application to Android." There you can find a lot of information about how to get your application ready for Android, as well as an example how to get the application running on mobile. There are also some workarounds explained for when you run into some specific problems.

Some things that I can share with you right now are that if you click the green button and you are not able to see your device, you might need to check a checkbox on your device to confirm that you allow your PC to have access to your phone. If you do not get a dialogue box or conformation dialogue, you might need to go to your device settings and enable developer mode. This can be done through a variety of ways, so google how it is supposed to work for your device. After you have done that rerun the application.

If your device does not pop up in the compatible device list, you might need to choose a different kit to run your application. This is because there are a few different types of Android devices out there. Choose the one you need and then run the application under that kit. Which kit you need can be found right under your device name. On the next screenshot you can see what everything should look like when it works.

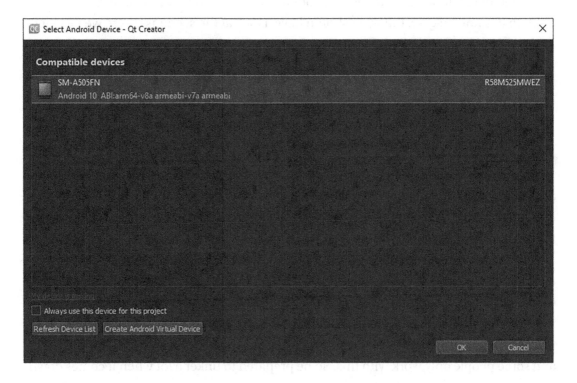

Select Android Device for deployment

This will open a new pop-up that allows us to select the device we want to use. At this point you should see a few permission requests on your mobile device. You need to allow all of them. When you have done this, you can click ok and the application will start building.

If your mobile device is not showing up here, you need to select a different kit under the Projects tab. Usually, you can see the kit you require in the Device list. But if this is not the case, then just try all out.

BUILD SUCCESSFUL in 17s

26 actionable tasks: 26 executed

Android package built successfully in 22.233 ms.

*-- File: D:/qtDev/build-Hang-Man-Android_Qt_6_0_0_Clang_
armeabi_v7a-Debug/android-build//build/outputs/apk/
debug/android-build-debug.apk*

When you set up everything correctly, you can see this in the compile console. With this the application will now deploy on your device and start up immediately.

If that is not the case, then you should have a look at the sections where we installed Android Studio and installed the NDK and SDK.

Android package built successfully in 22.233 ms.

*-- File: D:/qtDev/build-Hang-Man-Android_Qt_6_0_0_Clang_
armeabi_v7a-Debug/android-build//build/outputs/apk/
debug/android-build-debug.apk*

Also, if you want to publish your application on one of the many Play Stores or App Stores, you need the APK or APP file for that, which can be found in the build directory of our application. The link to this file can also be found in the console, so just grab it from there if you want to.

We are now done with deploying our application to a mobile device. We have our app deployed, it works, and we have created an APK file we could publish to all the different platforms out there, if they match the kit and are Android.

But believe me when I tell you that there is a lot more that you could and maybe need to do when you want to publish for a mobile device. The topic is large and complicated, and some people only work with this. So be prepared to tinker a lot when it comes down to deploying your application on your target device.

Also, for the Google Play Store you need a few specific settings to publish. First you need an APP file, which is a simple file that combines all the four different APK files you could create into one file that you can then publish to the Play Store. Also, the permissions you use may require special explanations on the Play Store, as Android is not too keen on giving out permissions to any unapproved application.

2.4.2.6 What We Learned

As always, we now should have a look at what we learned in this project. First we did a few things that are identical to the first project, like the Load and Main Page setup, which were repeated to learn them better.

But what new things did we learn? Here we will let us list what we did:

- **Grid View**

  We already used List Views a few times, and in this application we used List Views two times to achieve a specific visual component. The Grid View is not so different compared to the List View, but it has a totally different usage, and that is why we used it for the input of the different letters. There are also different ways of displaying and using the letters, but I prefer the Grid View for this.

- **Custom Components**

  We learned about setting up custom components, how to create them, and how to best use them. This is one of the things you will tend to do a lot when you create different applications on your own. As this is a thing you will do all the time it is not too hard to set up or to use, but it is a nice way of training yourself to use them.

- **Deploying to a Mobile Device**

  Learning how to build an application is one thing, but understanding how to deploy it to the desired platform is a totally different beast.

  It is not as hard to do, but there are not many tutorials about this topic. This is because the deploying of an application is always the last step in any development, and therefore it is the least interesting and least covered topic. I really hope you learned how to do this, and if so, you should be able to do this on your own from now on.

As you can see, we learned a few things in this project. Some of these are extremely important for development in general, others only if you are interested in the specific topic. Nevertheless, you need to repeat and use the now learned knowledge to keep it up to date.

2.4.3 Rock-Paper-Scissors Game

We already created two different applications, the Task-Master and the Hang-Man Game. Both taught us how to use different components and elements Qt offers and that you need to use all the time.

In this section we are going to create a Rock-Paper-Scissors Game. This will not more difficult than the previous example, but we are going to focus again on a game loop and on the visual components. Again, the main point with this is just to teach you a little bit more about Qt and how to use it.

2.4.3.1 Project Creation

As always, we start by creating our project. This time I am also going to cover the use of Git. All parts that revolve around the use of Git in our Project will be marked, and you do not need to follow them to understand the project, but I want to keep them in as I believe it can help a few people working with Git and Qt in conjunction.

Open up Qt Creator and let us start.

We are again choosing Qt Quick Application - Empty as our development template, because this is the template we are now most familiar with and because we do not need anything new or different in the template to get started. When you click on the correct template you can click Choose and continue.

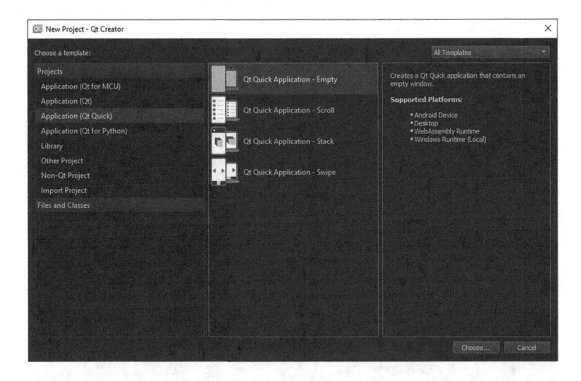

For the name of the application I have gone with Rock-Paper-Scissors_Game, because it fits what we are doing and describes what the application is going to be. Also, for the location the same limitations are valid as always.

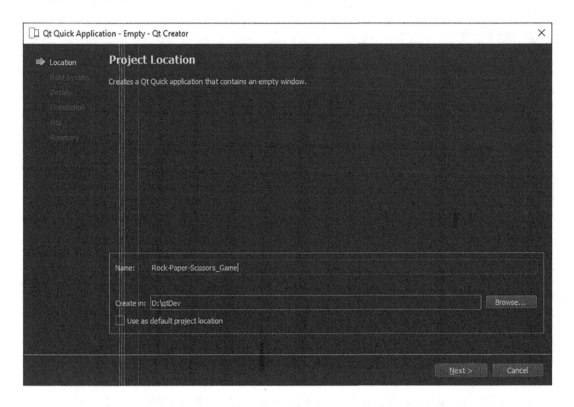

The build system as well as the minimal Qt Version we need stay the same as before. We do not need anything new here, but if you are a little rusty with what they mean, review the section with the first few steps with Qt.

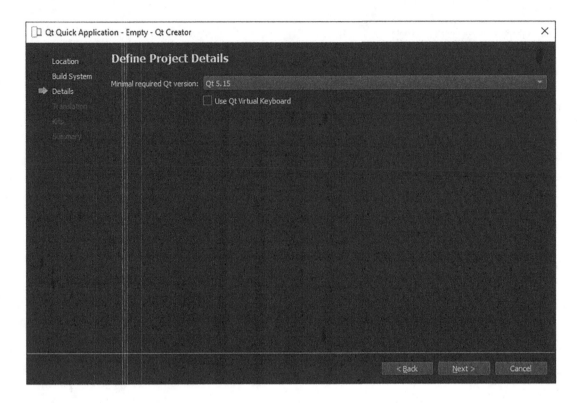

A translation file is again not required, but it is recommended if you were to build an application to a finished point.

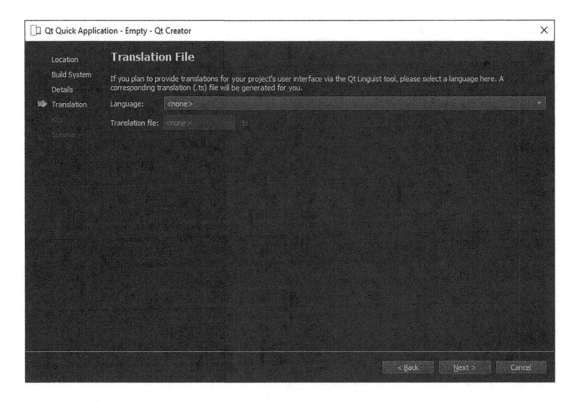

For simplicity, I am only choosing MinGW 64-bit as my Kit, only for the reason that that is the kit I am using to develop the application on.

As already mentioned, this is the main kit we used in our development of both the previous projects. If you did not choose this because you require another kit then choose that instead. The kit is really not that important for us.

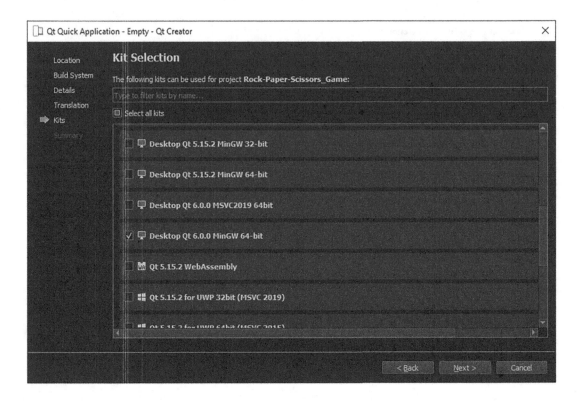

But for the final deployment, we are going to use the Android kit we already used in our previous application.

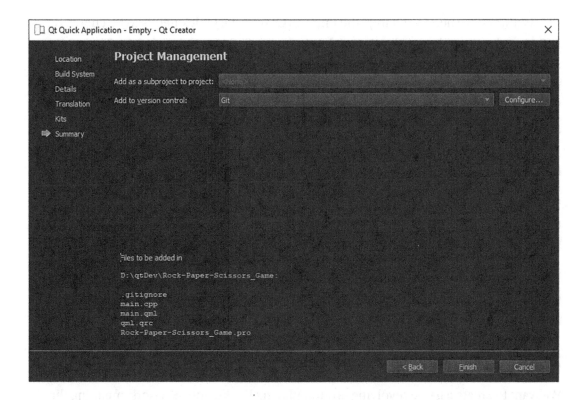

Finally, there is the most important page in the project creation wizard, and the only page that we have any notable changes on. Here you can see that we changed the version control to Git. Normally we left this empty, but because I want to show you a little how Qt works with Git, we are turning it on now. If you do not want to use Git here, you can also leave it out and skip the parts later on when we actually use it.

Simple ApplicationWindow with correct imports

```
1    import QtQuick 2.9
2    import QtQuick.Controls 2.5
3
4    ApplicationWindow {
5    width: 360
6    height: 640
7    visible: true
8    title: "Rock-Paper-Scissors"
9    }
```

As always, we need to change the imports Qt uses: Qt Quick needs to be changed to 2.15 and we can change the Qt Quick.Window to QtQuick.Controls 2.12. These are the basic things we always need for a normal functional application. We also can immediately change the Window component to an Application Window component. Inside here we can change the title to something a little bit more fitting like *Rock-Paper-Scissors Game.*

We are going to create a Mobile Application, so we can also change the width and height of the application to fit a mobile aspect ratio a little bit better.

```
5    width: 360
6    height: 640
```

As we are creating a Mobile Application, we can ignore creating a Load- and Main-Page setup, because we can use the splash screen Android provides us with. Now that we are done with creating the project, we can have a look at how the application should function.

2.4.3.2 Functionality

We want to create a game revolving around playing Rock-Paper-Scissors, meaning that we have a player as well as a bot playing against each other. Each round the player gets to choose between rock, paper, and scissors. Then the bot chooses randomly one of the three and they are compared. In the most basic Rock-Paper-Scissor game rules, paper beats rock, rock beats scissors, and scissors beats paper (other options will not be used here).

Here are the other things we need:

- Basic Rock-Paper-Scissors game rules

- Game-Loop from start to finish

- Animations that show how the game is progressing

- Win-loss point system

- The ability for win-loss points to be saved locally

Let us have a look at the diagram of our application, which will help clear up how this should all work. You can refer back to this point whenever you are not sure how we want to do things or if you do not understand why I do certain things.

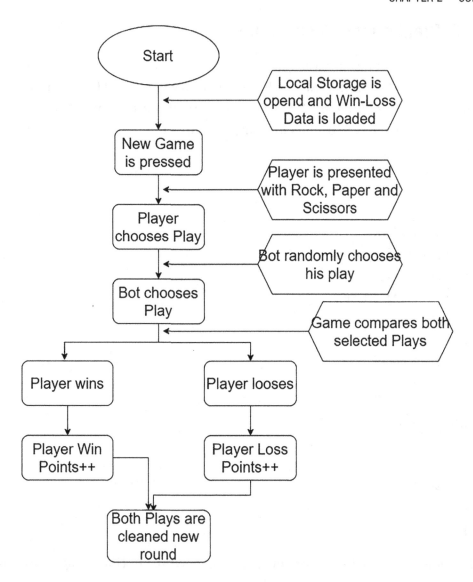

Diagram for the Rock-Paper-Scissors Game

As you can see the structure of the game could be called simple, but it will help us practice what we have learned and show you different ways to create applications.

2.4.3.3 Creating the Basic Game

We can start out creating our basic game by creating a Swipe View and putting three items inside of it. The Swipe View should have an id, a width, and a height that can be derived from *anchors.fill: parent*. We also need a currentIndex, so that while developing we can switch to 0, 1, or 2 to be directly transported to the corresponding Item inside of our Swipe View.

Simple Swipe View

```
10    SwipeView{
11    id: swipeView
12    anchors.fill: parent
13    currentIndex: 0
14    interactive: false
15
16    Item{
17    id: home_page
18    }
19    Item{
20    id: game_page
21    }
22    Item{
23    id: end_page
24    }
25    }
```

The items we should have inside of our Swipe View are our Home_Page, which is going to be just a page with a button in the middle to start the game. This is nothing special but it is a must-have, so that your players know what is going on.

As it is right now, we would have all the items and pages in one file. This is not really that great, because of readability and because it is extremely hard to keep track of what is going on if you have everything in one file. So let us separate our items.

This can be done as we have done a few times before. We are going to create three files, each for a corresponding page. You need to right-click on our qml.qrc folder and then select Add New, which will open up our New File Wizard.

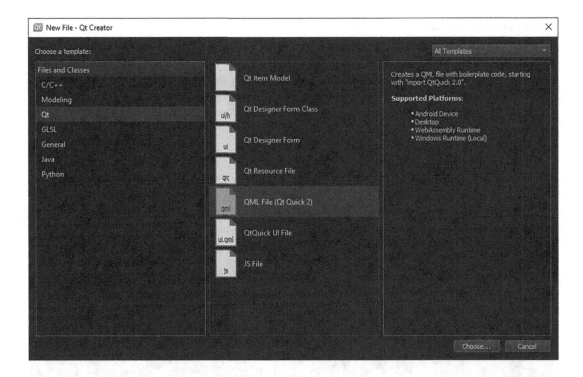

Here we are going to select QML File as our new file. When you have done that you can click Choose, which will open up the next page in the wizard. Here you can give our files a name. In our case we can use the id of our items we have in our main.qml.

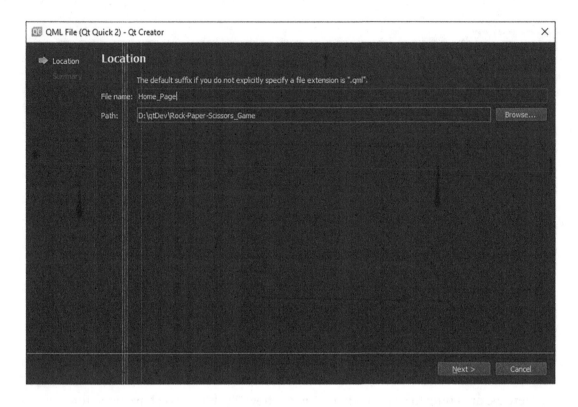

The path for our file can be the project location. If you have everything as mentioned you can click Next and we can continue.

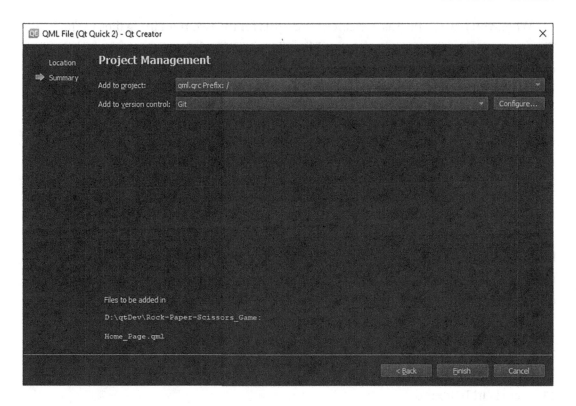

Lastly, we come to the page where Qt asks us where in the project we want to add this file, but because we do not have any sort of project structure at the moment, we can just leave everything as it is. It is important to mention that Add to version control should be Git, as we are going to Git later on.

```
1   import QtQuick 2.9
2   import QtQuick.Controls 2.5
3
4   Item{
5   id: home_page
6   width: 360
7   height: 640
```

To clean up a bit, we can change the code in our newly created file. We can more or less copy and paste the item we had in our Swipe View corresponding to the name of the file inside the file. We should also update the imports to the same as we have currently in our main.qml.

When you have done this, we can now do this for the two remaining files we need. The process is the exact same and should not be too difficult for you, but if it is then you can follow the way we did it for Home_Page.

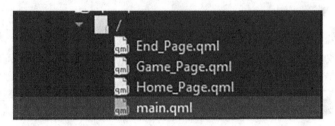

When you have done everything the same as the first file you should be left with three newly added files in our qml.qrc directory. The code in all of them should be more or less exactly the same, with the only difference being that the ids of the items are different.

```
10   SwipeView{
11   id: swipeView
12   anchors.fill: parent
13   currentIndex: 0
14   interactive: false
15
16   Home_Page{
17   id: home_page
18   }
19   Game_Page{
20   id: game_page
21   }
22   End_Page{
23   id: end_page
24   }
25   }
```

Lastly, we can change our main.qml a little, and the items of our Swipe View can be changed to the corresponding name of the Files we just created. This will immediately link them together and we can then use them.

I left the id as well as width and height of our items as they are and only changed the name of the component. This was because the Swipe View requires that the items inside of it to have a fixed width and height, and it also means that we did not need to change so much code.

2.4.3.4 Adding the Project to Git

We are now going to add this project to Git. This is a good example how this is done in Qt, and you can refer back to this when you create your own projects later.

The first thing you need to do is open up the project directory on your drive.

Name	Date modified	Type	Size
android	11/02/2021 19:42	File folder	
.gitignore	08/02/2021 14:23	Git Ignore-Quelld...	1 KB
Database	09/02/2021 19:52	JavaScript File	2 KB
drawImg	08/02/2021 21:06	PNG File	2 KB
End_Page	21/02/2021 18:42	Qt Quick Markup I...	1 KB
Game_Page	21/02/2021 18:41	Qt Quick Markup I...	1 KB
Home_Page	21/02/2021 18:40	Qt Quick Markup I...	2 KB
losImg	08/02/2021 21:06	PNG File	2 KB
main	08/02/2021 14:23	C++ Source file	1 KB
main	21/02/2021 18:44	Qt Quick Markup I...	1 KB
paperImg	08/02/2021 20:38	PNG File	1 KB
Player_Phase	21/02/2021 18:41	Qt Quick Markup I...	4 KB
qml.qrc	09/02/2021 18:53	QRC File	1 KB
Result_Phase	21/02/2021 18:41	Qt Quick Markup I...	2 KB
rockImg	08/02/2021 20:39	PNG File	3 KB
Rock-Paper-Scissors_Game	11/02/2021 19:42	Qt Project file	2 KB
Rock-Paper-Scissors_Game.pro.user	21/02/2021 18:44	VisualStudio.user....	43 KB
scissorImg	08/02/2021 20:39	PNG File	2 KB
winImg	08/02/2021 21:05	PNG File	1 KB

This should look kind of like this at the moment. As you can see there are all the files we created, as well as all the common Qt files that were created when we created the project.

Now that we are ready, there are a few ways to go about pushing this project to Git. Since they all start the same by opening up a Git Account, this is what we are going to do first. Google Git Hub and click on the first link that comes up.

github.com ▾ Diese Seite übersetzen

GitHub: Where the world builds software · GitHub

GitHub is where over 56 million developers shape the future of software, together. Contribute to the open source community, manage your Git repositories, ...

Ergebnisse von github.com	Q

Repositories
Fetch - Docs - ChooseALicense.com - Scientist - GitIgnore - Dmca

Codespaces
Your instant dev environment.

Explore
Explore is your guide to finding your next project, catching up ...

Features
Codespaces - Code review - Project management - Actions

Enterprise
Build like the best · Increase developer velocity. · Secure ...

Actions
Any language. GitHub Actions supports Node.js, Python, Java ...

Google search for Git Hub

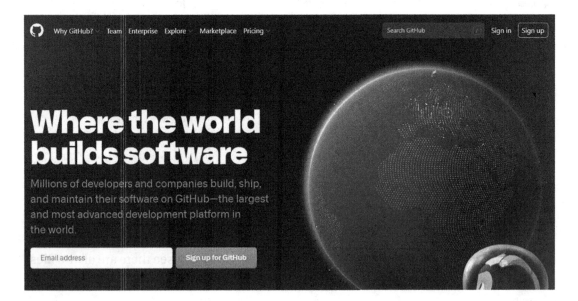

Git Hub homepage

Next you can click the Sign in or Sign-up buttons in the top left. I already have a Git Account, so I will sign in; if you do not already have one you can sign up. The sign-up process is not too difficult, so go ahead and do that.

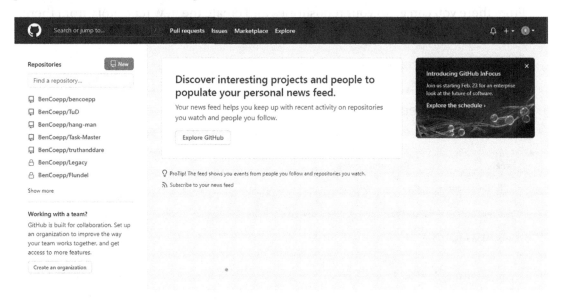

Git Hub logged in page

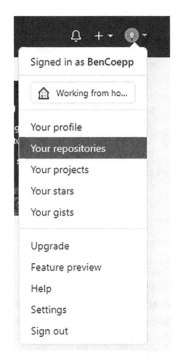

When you are signed in you should see this page. We now need to create a new repository, which you can do by using the green button in the top left with the bookmark, or when you click on your account profile icon, using the drop-down that opens up.

From there you can go to your repositories and create the new repository from there. For now, we can just click the green button on the left.[28]

A repository contains all project files, including the revision history. Already have a project repository elsewhere? Import a repository.

Create a new repository

Owner *   Repository name *

[BenCoepp ▾] / [   ]

Great repository names are short and memorable. Need inspiration? How about ubiquitous-octo-barnacle?

Description (optional)

[   ]

◉ Public
    Anyone on the internet can see this repository. You choose who can commit.

○ Private
    You choose who can see and commit to this repository.

Initialize this repository with:
Skip this step if you're importing an existing repository.

☐ Add a README file
    This is where you can write a long description for your project. Learn more.

☐ Add .gitignore
    Choose which files not to track from a list of templates. Learn more.

☐ Choose a license
    A license tells others what they can and can't do with your code. Learn more.

[Create repository]

---

[28] This might also be a good time to tell you to follow me on Git Hub. I tend to update already existing projects from time to time, and I will try to keep the projects covered in this book up to date to the book. Also, there might be some other projects or repositories that might interest you. I have developed quite a lot using Qt and some of the projects are already a few years old, but they might still be interesting for you.

This will transport us to a new page, where we need to fill out a few things. First we need to fill out the name for our repository. For us, a good name is *rock-paper-scissors_ game*.

Other the name we do not need anything else right now. You could change the repository to private if you do not want to make the repository visible for the entire Internet. After that you can click the green button at the bottom that says *Create repository*.

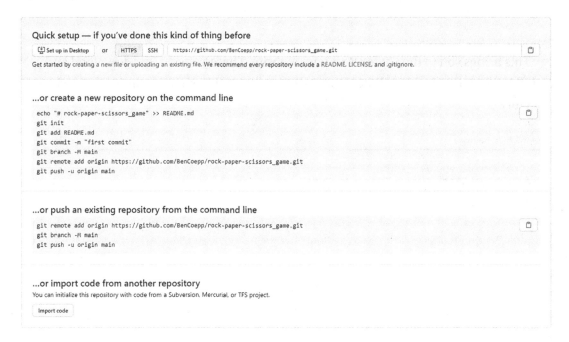

Guide to create a new repository, or adding a new repository

After a while of loading, you will be presented by this new page where you can see the commands we need so that our project is brought to Git Hub. As we already have a repository on our local machine (Qt always creates a repository for you when you create a project with version control enabled from the start), we need to use the second set of commands to get the project online. Getting the project online can be done in a few different ways, but the most standard and commonly used one is by Git Bash. If you do not have Git Bash, search for it online and choose the link in the next screenshot.

gitforwindows.org ▾ Diese Seite übersetzen

Git for Windows

Git BASH. Git for Windows provides a BASH emulation used to run Git from the command line. *NIX users should feel right at home, as the BASH ...

Andere suchten auch nach   ✕

tortoise git   git extensions

download nodejs for windows   git gui

gitlab windows   download tortoisegit windows 10

This brings you to the Git for Windows website. There you can just download and install Git for your machine. When you have installed Git Bash, you can open it up in the directory.

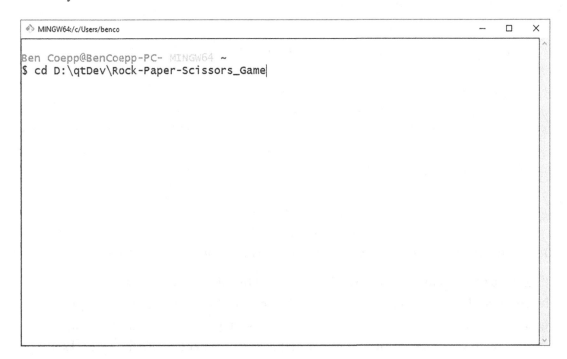

Going to the folder where we saved the project

Here you can see how to move to the correct folder using cd. You can see that you moved into the correct folder when you see a (master) on the right of the path.

```
MINGW64:/d/qtdev/Rock-Paper-Scissors_Game                                    —    □    ×

Ben Coepp@BenCoepp-PC- MINGW64 /d/qtdev/Rock-Paper-Scissors_Game (master)
$ git add .|
```

Adding all the newly created files

Next, we can use the command *git add* . This will stage all of the files we created with Qt, which you can imagine this like adding a lot of files to a list.

```
MINGW64:/d/qtdev/Rock-Paper-Scissors_Game                              —    □    ×

Ben Coepp@BenCoepp-PC- MINGW64 /d/qtdev/Rock-Paper-Scissors_Game (master)
$ git add .

Ben Coepp@BenCoepp-PC- MINGW64 /d/qtdev/Rock-Paper-Scissors_Game (master)
$ git commit -m"init commit|"
```

Committing all the files we just added

The next command we need to run is *git commit -m"commit msg"*, which will take the staged files and added a commit massage. This is now called a commit. This commit needs to be pushed now to Git Hub. In development we call this this *origin remote*.

I recommend that you try to keep the commit messages as professional and precise as you can. There is nothing more embarrassing for a developer than when your boss comes to you and tells you that commit *I like turtles* is not that professional.

Also, it is not possible to guess what the changes in the commit do by the name of it, so always say what you are doing in the commit so everyone knows what is going on.

```
MINGW64:/d/qtdev/Rock-Paper-Scissors_Game                                    —    □    ×

Ben Coepp@BenCoepp-PC- MINGW64 /d/qtdev/Rock-Paper-Scissors_Game (master)
$ git add .

Ben Coepp@BenCoepp-PC- MINGW64 /d/qtdev/Rock-Paper-Scissors_Game (master)
$ git commit -m"init commit"
[master (root-commit) 038a556] init commit
 8 files changed, 186 insertions(+)
 create mode 100644 .gitignore
 create mode 100644 End_Page.qml
 create mode 100644 Game_Page.qml
 create mode 100644 Home_Page.qml
 create mode 100644 Rock-Paper-Scissors_Game.pro
 create mode 100644 main.cpp
 create mode 100644 main.qml
 create mode 100644 qml.qrc

Ben Coepp@BenCoepp-PC- MINGW64 /d/qtdev/Rock-Paper-Scissors_Game (master)
$
```

Result of committing the files

```
MINGW64:/d/qtdev/Rock-Paper-Scissors_Game                                    —    □    ×

Ben Coepp@BenCoepp-PC- MINGW64 /d/qtdev/Rock-Paper-Scissors_Game (master)
$ git commit -m"init commit"
[master (root-commit) 038a556] init commit
 8 files changed, 186 insertions(+)
 create mode 100644 .gitignore
 create mode 100644 End_Page.qml
 create mode 100644 Game_Page.qml
 create mode 100644 Home_Page.qml
 create mode 100644 Rock-Paper-Scissors_Game.pro
 create mode 100644 main.cpp
 create mode 100644 main.qml
 create mode 100644 qml.qrc

Ben Coepp@BenCoepp-PC- MINGW64 /d/qtdev/Rock-Paper-Scissors_Game (master)
$ git push
fatal: The current branch master has no upstream branch.
To push the current branch and set the remote as upstream, use

    git push --set-upstream origin master

Ben Coepp@BenCoepp-PC- MINGW64 /d/qtdev/Rock-Paper-Scissors_Game (master)
$ |
```

Git push with fatal error

205

To upload the files to our remote, we need to run the command *git push*. This will not work yet, because when you push for the first time you need to clarify an upstream to the origin remote.

```
MINGW64:/d/qtdev/Rock-Paper-Scissors_Game                              —    □    ×

Ben Coepp@BenCoepp-PC- MINGW64 /d/qtdev/Rock-Paper-Scissors_Game (master)
$ git push
fatal: The current branch master has no upstream branch.
To push the current branch and set the remote as upstream, use

    git push --set-upstream origin master


Ben Coepp@BenCoepp-PC- MINGW64 /d/qtdev/Rock-Paper-Scissors_Game (master)
$ git push --set-upstream origin master
Enumerating objects: 10, done.
Counting objects: 100% (10/10), done.
Delta compression using up to 24 threads
Compressing objects: 100% (10/10), done.
Writing objects: 100% (10/10), 2.18 KiB | 2.18 MiB/s, done.
Total 10 (delta 1), reused 0 (delta 0), pack-reused 0
remote: Resolving deltas: 100% (1/1), done.
To https://github.com/BenCoepp/rock-paper-scissors_game.git
 * [new branch]      master -> master
Branch 'master' set up to track remote branch 'master' from 'origin'.

Ben Coepp@BenCoepp-PC- MINGW64 /d/qtdev/Rock-Paper-Scissors_Game (master)
$
```

Successful git push

You can just copy and paste the command that git tells you to run. It may be that a dialog box opens that asks you to log in with your Git Hub credentials. When your login credentials are correct the push will start and the project will be uploaded to Git Hub. When it tells you that it is done, you can go back to the site of Git we had open and when you reload it, you can see all the newly added files.

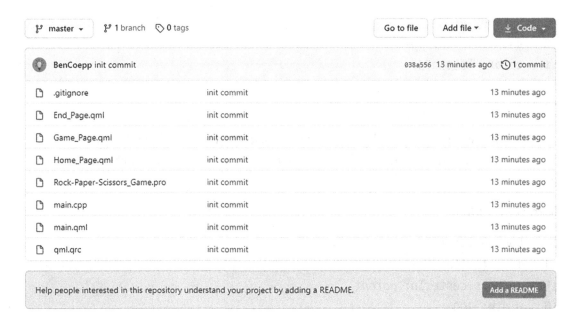

On Git Hub project site

With this, our project is now online on Git Hub. Later when we have created a few more files and changed others, we are going to open Git Bash again and push the new files and changes to Git Hub. But for now, let us continue with the development of the application.

2.4.3.5 Creating the Home Page

Go back to our newly created Home_Page.qml file. There we are going to create a rectangle as our background component.

Simple Home_Page.qml

```
1    import QtQuick 2.15
2    import QtQuick.Controls 2.12
3
4    Item{
5    id: home_page
6    width: 360
7    height: 640
8
```

```
9   Rectangle{
10   anchors.fill: parent
11   color: "#3e5a79"
12   }
13   }
```

The color we used here is the same that we have used throughout all of our applications until this point. Next, we can create the button through which we can start the game.

Start game button

```
13   RoundButton{
14   id: startGameBt
15   anchors.centerIn: parent
16   width: 200
17   text: "Start Game"
18   background: Rectangle{
19   anchors.fill: parent
20   radius: 99
21   color: "#fd7e35"
22   border.width: 1
23   }
24   onClicked: {
25   swipeView.setCurrentIndex(1)
26   }
27   }
```

The button we have here is similar to the ones we have created so far: we have an id, an anchor to center the button on the screen, and a background component so that we can have a slightly customized button. Lastly, we have our onClicked event that switches to the next Page in our Application.

Properties winCount and losCount

```
4   ApplicationWindow {
5   width: 360
6   height: 640
7   visible: true
```

```
 8   title: "Rock-Paper-Scissors"

 9

10   property var winCount: 0
11   property var losCount: 0
```

To make our Home_Page a little bit more interesting we can represent the win and loss counter on the page. First we need to add two properties to our main.qml file; they need to be available to the entire page, and the best way to do that is declaring them in our main.qml.

Next, we can create a label inside of our Home_Page.qml. The text should be white to be readable on the relatively dark background, and we should bin the label to the bottom center of our page, using *anchors.bottom: parent.bottom* and *horizontal.center: parent-horizontalCenter*.

Win and loss counter output

```
28   Label{
29   anchors.bottom: parent.bottom
30   anchors.horizontalCenter: parent.horizontalCenter
31   color: "white"
32   font.bold: true
33   text: "Win:: "+ winCount +" | "+ losCount+" ::Loss"
34   }
```

The only thing really missing on the Home_Page now is the title of our application. The label is not too difficult: we center it to the top and horizontal center and then give it a top margin so that it is not right up at the top, and it should be also white to be better readable and the font size should be around 25 so that it is readable even from afar.

Titel Label

```
14   Label{
15   anchors.horizontalCenter: parent.horizontalCenter
16   anchors.top: parent.top
17   anchors.topMargin: 100
18   text: "Rock-Paper-Scissor"
19   color: "white"
20   font.pointSize: 25
21   font.bold: true
22   }
```

Now if we were to run our application you will see that everything is rendered as it should be so far.

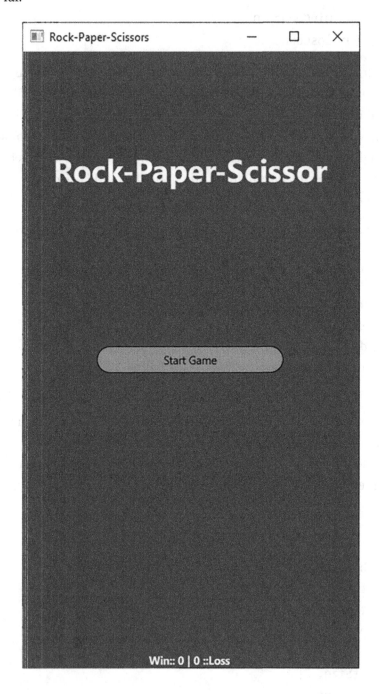

The only thing we should probably change is the button width and height, and the button should be round. I just find this aesthetically more pleasing; you might want to leave the button as it is.

Start Game button

```
24    RoundButton{
25    id: startGameBt
26    anchors.centerIn: parent
27    width: 200
28    height: 200
29    radius: 99
30    text: "Start Game"
31    background: Rectangle{
32    anchors.fill: parent
33    radius: 99
34    color: "#fd7e35"
35    border.width: 1
36    }
37    onClicked: {
38    swipeView.setCurrentIndex(1)
39    }
40    }
```

After the changes, our button should look something like this. Now we are more or less done with our Home_Page.qml. It is not a really difficult page and it did not take that much to pull off, but as always there is a lot more you could do such as adding animations or making everything a little bit prettier, but that is not our main mission here.

2.4.3.6 Creating the Game Page

The Game_Page will consist out of a Stack View, which will load the pages throughout the game loop. This is also where the functions for the game will be located. If you want to have a clearer overview of what the functionality should look like, you should review section 2.4.3.2, where we discussed how the game should work and function.

Game_Page.qml

```
1    import QtQuick 2.9
2    import QtQuick.Controls 2.5
3
4    Item{
5    id: game_page
6    width: 360
7    height: 640
8
9    Rectangle{
10   anchors.fill: parent
11   color: "#3e5a79"
12   }
13   }
```

First we can again update the imports, which needs to be done every time we have a new file.

Swipe View with Phases

```
14   SwipeView{
15   id: gameFrame
16   anchors.fill: parent
17   currentIndex: 0
18   interactive: false
19
20   Player_Phase{
21   id: playerPhase
22   width: 360
23   height: 640
24   }
25   Result_Phase{
26   id: resultPhase
27   width: 360
28   height: 640
29   }
30   }
```

Inside of our Game_Page we need to add a Swipe View, and that Swipe View needs an id so that we can interact with it later on, as well as an *anchors.fill: parent.* Inside of here we can now place these custom items inside the Swipe View. Since we do not have these yet, let us create them.

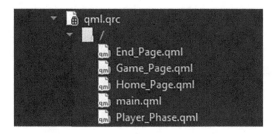

As we have already created multiple new pages throughout this book and two new ones in this section, I assume you will be able to create the Player_Phase.qml without any problems.

```
4    Item{
5    anchors.fill: parent
```

After you have created the file, you can go inside and we can start editing the code. Update the imports if you did not do this already. After that we can give the item an *acnhors.fill: parent* to make it responsive.

```
7    ListView{
8    id: optionListView
9    anchors.bottom: parent.bottom
10   height: 50
11   width: parent.width
12   orientation: ListView.Horizontal
```

Now we come to the real part of the application. We need to create a ListView here, which will be used to display the options the player has to choose from to play. In this case it might only be Rock, Paper, Scissor, but they need to be displayed so that the player can choose from them.

For the attributes, the ListView should be anchored to the bottom of our page, have a width that is identical to its parents, and a height of 50 should be enough for the icons. I also added the orientation property to our List View, which we used in the Hang-Man project. Here I do not want our items to be displayed vertically but horizontally, which in my opinion is just nicer to look at.

```
13    model: ListModel{
14    id: optionModel
15    ListElement{
16    img: "qrc:/rockImg.png"
17    value: ""
18    }
19    ListElement{
20    img: "qrc:/paperImg.png"
21    value: ""
22    }
23    ListElement{
24    img: "qrc:/scissorImg.png"
25    value: ""
26    }
27    }
```

Next, we can add our List Model to the corresponding model for our ListView. For now we only have three List Elements inside of our List Model. These are the options the player can choose from. Each List Element has two values inside of it: one is the actual value of the element, and the other is going to be a link to an image so we have a visual representation of the element.

This is not the best way of implementing all the different options we could have in our game, but it allows us to quite easily implement another option, delete one, or give the player the option to implement their own.

This is to be expected of the List Model we have here. You probably are already quite familiar with the different functionalities a List Model has to offer.

```
28    delegate: Item {
29    width: parent.width/3
30    height: parent.height
31
32    MouseArea{
33    anchors.centerIn: parent
34    width: 50
35    height: 50
36    onClicked: {
```

```
37    //function that starts the game
38    console.log(value)
39    }
40
41    Image {
42    anchors.fill: parent
43    antialiasing: true
44    source: img
45    }
46    }
47    }
```

The delegate also follows the List Models theme of being fairly simple. It consists of an item, and the width of this item should be a third of the width the parent has, so here it is width/3. The height can be the same as the parent's height.

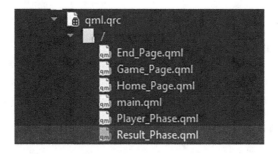

Inside of the item we are going to place a Mouse Area, which will fill the item and have a onClicked even inside of it. For now we will only have a simple console log where we print out the value of the item we clicked. Inside of this Mouse Area we can also place an image that can display the img data. We can fill its parent with the image and set antialiasing to true. The source of this image should be just img, as this will hold the data of the element.

As we are nearly done with the Player_Phase.qml, we can create Result_Phase.qml, which we have done multiple times already.

Next open up the Result_Phase.qml, and we can start editing the code. As always update the imports and add an *anchors.fill: parent* to the Item already present in the file. Next, we can add the first real component to the item, a Mouse Area.

The Mouse Area should have a width and height of 50 for now, and it should be cantered on the screen. We can also add the onClicked event for this Mouse Area. In

215

this case we can immediately tell the gameFrame, which is the second Swipe View we created, to go back to the first item or just index 0. This can be best done through the *.setCurrentIndex()* method.

Inside this Mouse Area we can also add another Image, which is filling the Mouse Area and has for now an empty source property.

```
1   import QtQuick 2.9
2   import QtQuick.Controls 2.5
3
4   Item{
5   Anchors.fill: parent
6
7   MouseArea{
8   anchors.centerIn: parent
9   width: 50
10  height: 50
11  onClicked: {
12  swipeView.setCurrentIndex(0)
13  }
14  Image{
15  anchors.fill: parent
16  antialiasing: true
17  source: "file"
18  }
19  }
20
21  Label{
22  anchors.bottom: parent.bottom
23  anchors.horizontalCenter: parent.horizontalCenter
24  color: "white"
25  font.bold: true
26  text: "Win:: "+ winCount +" | "+ losCount+" ::Loss"
27  }
28  }
```

Below the Mouse Area we can add a label. This label should display the current wins and losses of the player. If you do not want to type everything out, you can go to the Home_Page and copy the Label from there and only change the properties you need here. Other than that, we position this label also to the bottom of our page, but give it a bottom margin and push it a little higher.

```
32   MouseArea{
33   anchors.fill: parent
34   onClicked: {
35   //function that starts the game
36   Console.log(value)
37   swipeView.setCurrentIndex(1)
38   }
39   }
```

Now we can also change the onClicked function in our Player_Phase.qml file a little. For now, we can just add *gameFrame.setCurrentIndex(1)*. We need this to change the page of the Swipe View.

playerOption and botOpton added to Game_Page.qml

```
4    Item{
5    id: game_page
6    width: 360
7    height: 640
8
9    property var playerOption: ""
10   property var botOption: ""
```

Inside of our Game_Page.qml we can add two properties. The first one is the playerOption and the botOption. They will hold the option that they for instance the player has made.

```
32   MouseArea{
33   anchors.centerIn: parent
34   width: 50
35   height: 50
36   onClicked: {
37   //function that starts the game
```

```
38    console.log(value)
39    gameFrame.setCurrentIndex(1)
40    playerOption = value
41    botOption = optionModel.get(Math.floor(Math.random() * optionModel.
      count))
42    }
```

Now to the real fun of our application, go back to our Player_Phase.qml and let us change the onClicked event a little.

First we can add that the playerOption should be the value we clicked. That is pretty straightforward and understandable. To set the botOption we need a little bit more code. We can get a random Item from our optionModel. The function you see in the brackets is basic JavaScript. We generate a random number and that is then going to be the botOption.

```
50    function winCheck(){
51    if(playerOption === botOption.value){
52    //draw
53    }else if(playerOption === "rock" && botOption.value === "scissor"){
54    //player win
55    }else if(playerOption === "paper" && botOption.value === "scissor"){
56    //player win
57    }else if(playerOption === "paper" && botOption.value === "rock"){
58    //player win
59    }else if(playerOption === "scissor" && botOption.value === "rock"){
60    //bot win
61    }else if(playerOption === "scissor" && botOption.value === "paper"){
62    //player win
63    }else if(playerOption === "rock" && botOption.value === "paper"){
64    //bot win
65    }
66    }
```

Now that we have a player and bot Option, we can write our winCheck function. For now, this can just be an extremely ugly if-else statement that just checks all the possible variants of rock, paper, and scissor.

```
50    function winCheck(){
51    if(playerOption === botOption.value){
52    //draw
53    }else if(playerOption === "rock" && botOption.value === "scissor"){
54    //player win
55    winCount++
56    }else if(playerOption === "paper" && botOption.value === "scissor"){
57    //player win
58    winCount++
59    }else if(playerOption === "paper" && botOption.value === "rock"){
60    //player win
61    winCount++
62    }else if(playerOption === "scissor" && botOption.value === "rock"){
63    //bot win
64    losCount++
65    }else if(playerOption === "scissor" && botOption.value === "paper"){
66    //player win
67    winCount++
68    }else if(playerOption === "rock" && botOption.value === "paper"){
69    //bot win
70    losCount++
71    }
72    gameFrame.setCurrentIndex(1)
73    //upload to local storage
74    }
```

We also can add the basic functionality of increasing the loss and win count. This can be easily done by just using the ++ operator and increasing the number by 1.

At the bottom of the long if-else statement we can add the change of the gameFrame index. When the function finishes, the player is transported to the Result_Phase of our Application.

```
9     property var playerOption: ""
10    property var botOption: ""
11    property var winState: 0 //0=draw 1=player Win 2=player los
```

Next, we can add another property to our Game_Page, the winState property. For now, this property should be initialized with 0, and on the right of that you can see a comment where I list the other possibilities this property can have.

```
14    Image {
15    anchors.fill: parent
16    antialiasing: true
17    source: if(winState===0){}
18    else if(winState===1){}
19    else if(winState===2){}
20    }
```

The image on our Result_Phase currently does not have anything as its source, but we cannot put anything in there that is fixed. We need to write a function as the source, for when the winState represents a value a specific image will be placed as the image source. It is a really simple function, but not the most elegant way to build this functionality.

```
11    onClicked: {
12    gameFrame.setCurrentIndex(0)
13    winState = 0
14    playerOption = ""
15    botOption = ""
16    }
```

Above the image we had our onClicked function that was relatively empty, so let us add a few more things to the event. When the player clicks this Mouse Area the winner was already selected and displayed, so we can empty all of the properties we have. This is not really necessary in this case, but I prefer to empty properties that get different values next time.

```
36    Timer{
37    id: resultTimer
38    interval: 10000
39    repeat: false
40    running: false
41    onTriggered: {
42    gameFrame.setCurrentIndex(0)
```

```
43    winState = 0
44    playerOption = ""
45    botOption = ""
46    }
47    }
```

Below all of the components we added so far, we can also add a timer component. This is a component we did not have so far, so let me explain what it is.

A timer can be best described as a clock that ticks down time you set in its interval property, and when the time is up you get an onTriggered even and then you can run a function. This is extremely great when you want to trigger certain behavior in your application in a time-based frame.

Why do I want to use this here? Well, when the player gets to the result phase, he has the option to click the image and get back to the Player_Phase page, but maybe they do not want to click there. I do not want the player just sitting there the entire time, so when this timer is up the same functions are going to be run as when the player clicks the Mouse Area.

```
17    Image {
18    anchors.fill: parent
19    antialiasing: true
20    source: if(winState===0){}
21    else if(winState===1){}
22    else if(winState===2){}
23    onSourceChanged: {
24    resultTimer.start()
25    }
26    }
```

A small problem we have here is that the timer will not start immediately when we come to this page. The best way to start the timer is by listening to the source change event of our image. This will trigger when the player comes to this page and the winState is not 0, and when that is the case there is no change in the source of the image as the source was already there. But if it is anything else then the source will be changed and the timer can then be started right away. This is a fairly nice way of doing something like this.

221

Now that we are done with the functionality, we can go and grab some icons for our Rock, Paper, and Scissors. I got mine online, and if you want to get the same then look at the Git Repository, where you will find all the images you will need.

I choose these images because I like them and they fit the style I am going for, but as always, it is not about how they look and I only want them to represent the value.[29]

More useful to know than which images I choose is how to get images into your project. I will now present you with the fastest and easiest way I know to get them in your project, which is not the best or nicest way, but I prefer it for its simplicity.

Before we can start importing the images into our project, you should have downloaded all the images we need into our project by dumping them into the project folder.

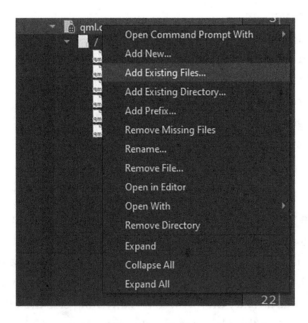

---

[29] I made these icons myself using inspiration online. There are a lot of better ones out there, but I wanted to do them myself.

Now that you have all the images in the project directory, let us import them into our project. For that you should right-click the qml.qrc directory in our project tree and then select the Add Existing File. This will open up an explorer, which should automatically show the project directory, and here you need to select all the images you want.

Name	Date modified	Type	Size
android	11/02/2021 19:42	File folder	
.gitignore	08/02/2021 14:23	Git Ignore-Quelld...	1 KB
Database	09/02/2021 19:52	JavaScript File	2 KB
drawImg	08/02/2021 21:06	PNG File	2 KB
End_Page	21/02/2021 18:42	Qt Quick Markup I...	1 KB
Game_Page	21/02/2021 18:41	Qt Quick Markup I...	1 KB
Home_Page	21/02/2021 18:40	Qt Quick Markup I...	2 KB
losImg	08/02/2021 21:06	PNG File	2 KB
main	08/02/2021 14:23	C++ Source file	1 KB
main	21/02/2021 18:44	Qt Quick Markup I...	1 KB
paperImg	08/02/2021 20:38	PNG File	1 KB
Player_Phase	21/02/2021 18:41	Qt Quick Markup I...	4 KB
qml.qrc	09/02/2021 18:53	QRC File	1 KB
Result_Phase	21/02/2021 20:31	Qt Quick Markup I...	2 KB
rockImg	08/02/2021 20:39	PNG File	3 KB
Rock-Paper-Scissors_Game	11/02/2021 19:42	Qt Project file	2 KB
Rock-Paper-Scissors_Game.pro.user	21/02/2021 18:44	VisualStudio.user....	43 KB
scissorImg	08/02/2021 20:39	PNG File	2 KB
winImg	08/02/2021 21:05	PNG File	1 KB

When you have selected them, you can click open. This will lead to the explorer closing.

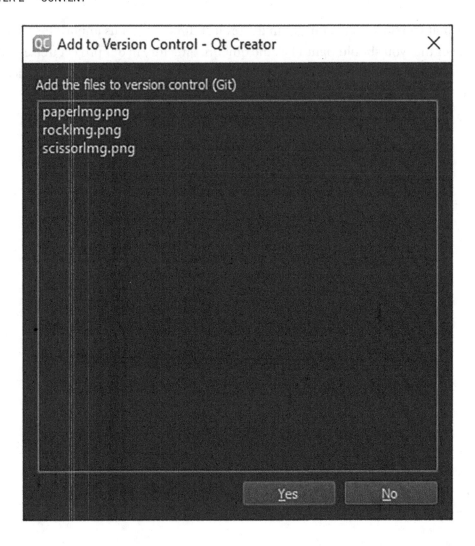

Images that are going to be added

When you have Git enabled this pop-up will open. For all external files you add to your project tree, Qt will ask you if you want to add them to your version control. In our case I will choose yes, as I want these images in my Git Repository. In most cases you will probably also click yes.

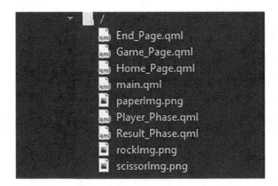

When everything has been done correctly you will have a few new files in your project directory. You may think that this looks extremely unorganized, but we are going to fix this later on.

```
13    model: ListModel{
14    id: optionModel
15    ListElement{
16    img: "qrc:/rockImg.png"
17    value: "rock"
18    }
19    ListElement{
20    img: "qrc:/paperImg.png"
21    value: "paper"
22    }
23    ListElement{
24    img: "qrc:/scissorImg.png"
25    value: "scissor"
26    }
27    }
```

Now that we have all the images in our project, we can add them to the places we need them. The first place is in our options List Model. There we can add the corresponding images to the corresponding value and place them in the img property.

```
32    MouseArea{
33    anchors.centerIn: parent
34    width: 50
35    height: 50
```

```
36    onClicked: {
37    //function that starts the game
38    console.log(value)
39    gameFrame.setCurrentIndex(1)
40    playerOption = value
41    botOption = optionModel.get(Math.floor(Math.random() * optionModel.
      count))
42    winCheck()
43    }
```

Next, we can add our nearly finished winCheck function to our Mouse Areas onClicked event. Every time we click the Mouse Area we are moved to the next page and our winCheck function tells us who the winner is.

```
18    SwipeView{
19    id: gameFrame
20    anchors.fill: parent
21    currentIndex: 0
22    interactive: false
```

A small problem that we should also fix right at this point is the fact that if you were to run our application now, you would see that you can still swipe our Swipe View, which completely breaks our application. To stop this from happening we can just add the *interactive: false* attribute to both our Swipe Views.

```
13    SwipeView{
14    id: gameFrame
15    anchors.fill: parent
16    currentIndex: 0
17    interactive: false
```

Next, we can have a look at the currently empty Image on our Result_Phase.qml page. We already built the function that takes the winState and then adjusts the image according to that, but we do not have any images for it right now.

The images you can see here are the ones that I will use for this purpose.[30] We have a check icon for when you won, a warning sign for when you lost, and a balance for when you got a draw.

As before, we add these images by adding them as existing files, which will open up the explorer where you need to select all the images you want to import. When you have done that you can click open and the pop-up will open again.

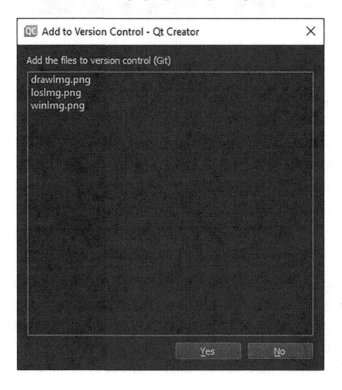

We can now add all the images to our version control, and when you have done that and clicked yes, you will see that the new images were added to our project tree. Now it looks even worse than before.

---

[30] These images were again made by myself, and you can find them in the repository on Git Hub.

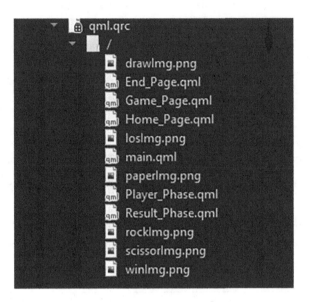

```
16    Image {
17    anchors.fill: parent
18    antialiasing: true
19    source: if(winState===0){"qrc:/drawImg.png"}
20    else if(winState===1){"qrc:/winImg.png"}
21    else if(winState===2){"qrc:/losImg.png"}
22    onSourceChanged: {
23    resultTimer.start()
24    }
25    }
```

Now that we have imported our images, we can fill out the source function with the corresponding images. If you do not know how to get the URL of the image, then right-click the image in your project directory, where will be an option in the menu that opens up where you can do this.

Other than that, fill out the function with the URLs as you see in the preceding screenshot.

```
6    MouseArea{
7    width: 100
8    height: 100
9    anchors.centerIn: parent
```

A small change I made here is that I changed the size of the Mouse Area on our Result_Phase.qml to something a little bit larger. Other than that, we do not need to change too much here.

```
6    ListView{
7     id: optionListView
8     anchors.bottom: parent.bottom
9     anchors.bottomMargin: 50
10    height: 50
```

Also, I added a bottom margin to our option List View, just because it looks nicer and is a lot easier to read than before.

```
6    MouseArea{
7    anchors.centerIn: parent
8    width: 200
9    height: 200
10   onClicked: {
11   swipeView.setCurrentIndex(2)
12   }
13   Rectangle{
14   anchors.fill: parent
15   radius: 99
16   color: "#fd7e35"

17   Label{
18   anchors.centerIn: parent
19   font.bold: true
20   font.pointSize: 25
21   text: "Stop Game"
22   }
23   }
24   }
```

The last thing we need to do is add a stop game button to our Player_Phase.qml page. Currently there is no way to stop the game, which is not good, and we need to give the player the option to quit the game.

This can best be done by simply having a Mouse Area with a Rectangle inside of it and a Label inside of that. The label only needs to say that you can stop the game when you press there. This is nothing special, but it allows the user to see that the game can be closed.

2.4.3.7 Creating the End Page

```
1    import QtQuick 2.9
2    import QtQuick.Controls 2.5
3
4    Item{
5    id: end_page
6    width: 360
7    height: 640
8
9    Rectangle{
10   anchors.fill: parent
11   color: "#3e5a79"
12   }
13
14   Label{
15   anchors.bottom: parent.bottom
16   anchors.bottomMargin: 100
17   anchors.horizontalCenter: parent.horizontalCenter
18   color: "white"
19   font.bold: true
20   font.pointSize: 25
21   text: "Win:: "+ winCount +" | "+ losCount+" ::Loss"
22   }
23   }
```

First we need to change the End_Page.qml to look something like this. We have a Rectangle as our background component, and a label at the bottom of our screen that is more or less the same we used on the Home_Page.qml or Result_Phase.qml, only the position and size are a bit different.

After that we can add another Label above the first one we created. This will just tell the player that they played a good game, whether they win or lose.

```
9    Rectangle{
10     anchors.fill: parent
11     color: "#3e5a79"
12     }
13
14     Label{
15     anchors.top: parent.top
16     anchors.topMargin: 100
17     anchors.horizontalCenter: parent.horizontalCenter
18     color: "white"
19     font.bold: true
20     font.pointSize: 25
21     text: "Good Game!!"
22     }
```

This is a basic end page. In my opinion the best end pages are the ones that only tell you the bare minimum that is needed. Here we only have a label that tells you that you had a good game and below we have something that displays the score of the game, and that is it: a remarkably simple and clean end to our game.

Many people might want to make the End_Page a little bit prettier and make it stand out a bit more, but for what I was aiming for this was not necessary. It would be a good learning experience, however, so feel free to do this after this project if you want to.

And with that we are more or less done with the writing of our application, so let us have a look at what we did.

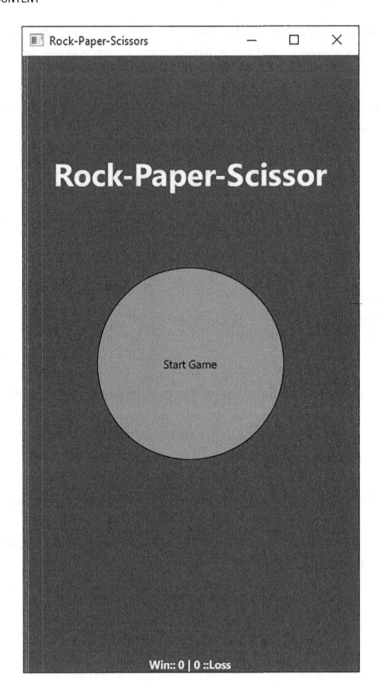

If you want to run the application, you can click the green arrow down in the left bottom. If you have done everything correctly so far, the application should run just like you saw right now.

The application in that sense is now finished and running, and we have made a Rock-Paper-Scissor game that could be considered finished.

At this point we can push our changes and new files to git, which means that even when something happens to your device you could just clone the repository remotely and access the project again.

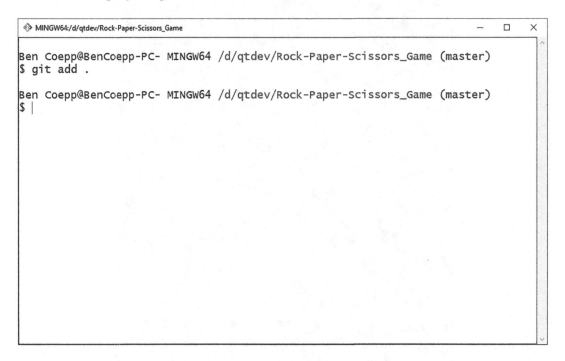

The first command we need to run is *git add* . , which will add up all the files and changes we did so far. If you want a full explanation of what git add . does you should see Chapter 3, section 3.2.3, "Git in Qt," where you will find a bit more information, but the best place to learn about Git is the Internet.

There are also a lot of really good books about Git out there, so feel free to get one of those as they are a great learning tool to understand Git a lot better.

```
MINGW64:/d/qtdev/Rock-Paper-Scissors_Game                              —    □    ×

Ben Coepp@BenCoepp-PC- MINGW64 /d/qtdev/Rock-Paper-Scissors_Game (master)
$ git add .

Ben Coepp@BenCoepp-PC- MINGW64 /d/qtdev/Rock-Paper-Scissors_Game (master)
$ git commit -m"added a lot of changes"
[master 6b61e92] added a lot of changes
 13 files changed, 263 insertions(+), 3 deletions(-)
 create mode 100644 Player_Phase.qml
 create mode 100644 Result_Phase.qml
 create mode 100644 drawImg.png
 create mode 100644 losImg.png
 create mode 100644 paperImg.png
 create mode 100644 rockImg.png
 create mode 100644 scissorImg.png
 create mode 100644 winImg.png

Ben Coepp@BenCoepp-PC- MINGW64 /d/qtdev/Rock-Paper-Scissors_Game (master)
$
```

The next command we can run is *git commit -m""*. This command takes all the added files and puts them in a commit with a commit massage to it.

As you can see here, I did not do a great job adding a specific commit message to it. Generally, you want to say extremely specifically what you did in your commit, which files you touched, and what changes you made. This makes it easy for people to understand what you did, but this is not the case in this example.

```
MINGW64:/d/qtdev/Rock-Paper-Scissors_Game                              —    □    ×

13 files changed, 263 insertions(+), 3 deletions(-)
create mode 100644 Player_Phase.qml
create mode 100644 Result_Phase.qml
create mode 100644 drawImg.png
create mode 100644 losImg.png
create mode 100644 paperImg.png
create mode 100644 rockImg.png
create mode 100644 scissorImg.png
create mode 100644 winImg.png

Ben Coepp@BenCoepp-PC- MINGW64 /d/qtdev/Rock-Paper-Scissors_Game (master)
$ git push
Enumerating objects: 21, done.
Counting objects: 100% (21/21), done.
Delta compression using up to 24 threads
Compressing objects: 100% (15/15), done.
Writing objects: 100% (15/15), 10.77 KiB | 5.38 MiB/s, done.
Total 15 (delta 2), reused 0 (delta 0), pack-reused 0
remote: Resolving deltas: 100% (2/2), completed with 1 local object.
To https://github.com/BenCoepp/rock-paper-scissors_game.git
   038a556..6b61e92  master -> master

Ben Coepp@BenCoepp-PC- MINGW64 /d/qtdev/Rock-Paper-Scissors_Game (master)
$ |
```

Lastly, we can run the *git push* command. This will push all our changes to Git Hub. And with that we are done with the basic creating of our application.

We now have a finished and functional app that looks terrible and has a terrible project structure, but it is functional. You can run it now and see for yourself, but I will not accept mediocrity, and I want something a little bit nicer.

2.4.3.8 Fixing the Mess

As you probably can see right now, the project has no structure, some functions like the winCheck function are needlessly long, and even worse, some parts of the application look downright horrendous.

This was intentional, because we always try to write and build great applications with great project structure and good written code, but that is not always the case, or our co-workers have done a terrible job. There will come the time where you need to polish an already existing project that is actually presentable, and that is what we are going to do next.

This section is somewhat optional, so if you do not want to do this then you can also skip this to the next section where we implement the local storage system.

The first thing we should have a look at here is the separation of images into a new prefix. This should be done for two reasons: it is far easier to read this than normally, and it also gives our project a lot more structure.

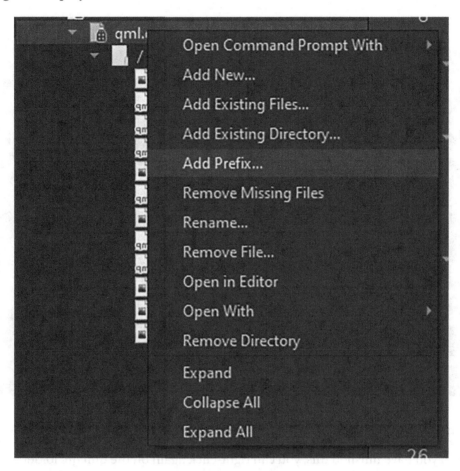

The first thing we need to do for that is adding a new prefix to our project. You can right-click qml.qrc and select the Add Prefix option.

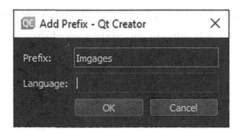

This will open up a wizard that will ask you for the name of the prefix you want to create as well as the language. Here we only need to fill out the name. I choose Images as the name for the prefix, but you can choose whatever you want. Click ok when you are done.

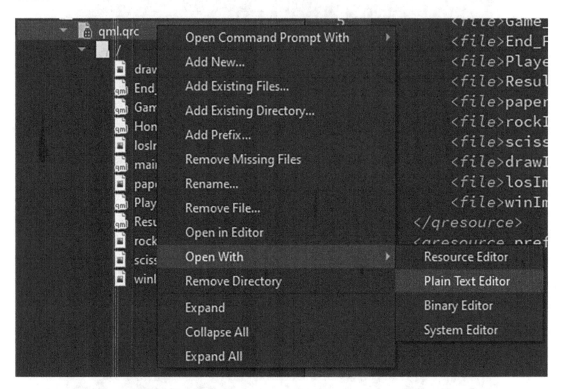

Opening the Plain Text Editor

When you have finished this, you can right-click again on the qml.qrc folder and open up the submenu Open With. Here you need to select Plain Text Editor, which we have not yet covered.

The other options you can see here in the submenu are also ways of opening up and editing the project structure. The one we used previously was the Resource Editor itself, but sometimes the best option is editing the plain text of the file. Open it up in Plain Text Editor.

```
 1 ▾   <RCC>
 2 ▾       <qresource prefix="/">
 3             <file>main.qml</file>
 4             <file>Home_Page.qml</file>
 5             <file>Game_Page.qml</file>
 6             <file>End_Page.qml</file>
 7             <file>Player_Phase.qml</file>
 8             <file>Result_Phase.qml</file>
 9             <file>paperImg.png</file>
10             <file>rockImg.png</file>
11             <file>scissorImg.png</file>
12             <file>drawImg.png</file>
13             <file>losImg.png</file>
14             <file>winImg.png</file>
15         </qresource>
16         <qresource prefix="/Imgages"/>
17   </RCC>
```

Plain Text Editor content

If you open it up it will look like this. We have all our files and images in the empty prefix up top and our newly created prefix just sitting empty down below.

```
1    <RCC>
2        <qresource prefix="/">
3            <file>main.qml</file>
4            <file>Home_Page.qml</file>
5            <file>Game_Page.qml</file>
6            <file>End_Page.qml</file>
7            <file>Player_Phase.qml</file>
8            <file>Result_Phase.qml</file>
9        </qresource>
10       <qresource prefix="/Imgages">
11           <file>paperImg.png</file>
12           <file>rockImg.png</file>
13           <file>scissorImg.png</file>
14           <file>drawImg.png</file>
15           <file>losImg.png</file>
16           <file>winImg.png</file>
17       </qresource>
18   </RCC>
```

Update resource in Plain Text Editor

The fastest way to change the project structure is to just rewrite the file a little, like you see in the preceding screenshot. We moved all the images down into the Images Prefix, and when you click save you will see this.

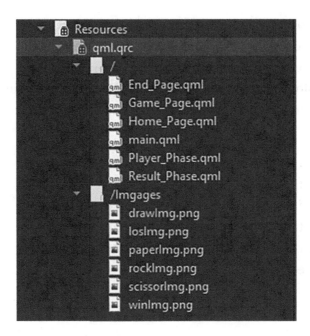

As you can see, there is an immediate improvement to our project structure. All the images are nicely located and ordered away from all other files, and it does not look so cluttered.

```
34    model: ListModel{
35    id: optionModel
36    ListElement{
37    img: "qrc:/Imagages/rockImg.png"
38    value: "rock"
39    }
40    ListElement{
41    img: "qrc:/ Imagages/paperImg.png"
42    value: "paper"
43    }
44    ListElement{
45    img: "qrc:/ Imagages/scissorImg.png"
46    value: "scissor"
47    }
48    }
```

But if you were to run the application now, you would get the error that the images are missing or not properly defined. This is because we changed the URL of the images. To fix this we need to add the new URL to the corresponding place.

For the optionModel you can see the correct URLs in the preceding screenshot, and for the Result_Phase ones you can have a look at the following screenshots:

```
16    Image {
17    anchors.fill: parent
18    antialiasing: true
19    source: if(winState===0){"qrc:/Imgages/drawImg.png"}
20    else if(winState===1){"qrc:/ Imgages/winImg.png"}
21    else if(winState===2){"qrc:/ Imgages/losImg.png"}
22    nSourceChanged: {
23    resultTimer.start()
24    }
25    }
```

Now that we are done with this, you can see a great improvement already, but let us not stop here. You might think that we can shrink the winCheck function, but unfortunately this is not really possible, mainly because of the many combinations we already have when we only have three options the player and bot can choose from.

But something we can improve a little and work on is the visual fidelity of our application. The first thing we can touch is on our Home_Page.qml.

```
30    font.bold: true
31    font.pointSize: 25
32    text: "Start Game"
```

Before we only had the text property, so the text was very plain and not that great. The best thing we can do to immediately improve the product is simply making the text bold and making it a bit bigger.

This greatly improves readability and makes it more visually stunning. The next thing we can touch on is also in this file.

```
43    Label{
44    anchors.bottom: parent.bottom
45    anchors.bottomMargin: 50
```

This is also a fairly quick fix: we add a margin to the bottom anchor, which means that the label that displays the win and loss of our player is a little bit better presented. It is a quite simple and quick fix, but it improves the product display.

The next thing we can add to improve the application is a label above our Mouse Area on our Result_Phase.qml. Currently there is nothing that tells the player that they should click the icon that is displayed here. The player will only know what to do if they know the game or if they by chance press the button.

```
4    Label{
5    anchors.top: parent.top
6    anchors.topMargin: 100
7    anchors.horizontalCenter: parent.horizontalCenter
```

```
8    color: "white"
9    font.bold: true
10   font.pointSize: 15
11   text: "Click the Icon" ::Loss"
12   }
```

Therefore, we can just add a label above our Mouse Area, center it to the top of our page, and give it a text that tells the player what to do. This is also a fairly quick fix, but it improves the understanding of the player a lot.

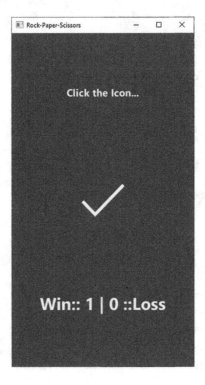

There are a lot of ways to tell the user what to do. One is through the use of text like we just did, which is the easiest and most understandable and the one that users are most familiar with. But you can also use color or composition of elements to guide the user into doing actions or moving through the application the way you want. These all rely on your understanding of how the user is going to operate. If you are interested in a subject like this, there are a lot of great topics and papers on the matter, though it is a topic we are not going to discuss too much in this game.

The last thing I want to improve is adding the check image we imported earlier to the End_Page.qml, because currently the End_Page.qml does not look that great and is a little empty. To change that, an image is a great solution.

```
24    Image {
25    anchors.centerIn: parent
26    width: 200
27    height: 200
28    antialiasing: true
29    source: "qrc:/Imgages/winImg.png"
30    }
```

You can just add this image below our label we created just a few pages back. The attributes the image has are the standard attributes you would suspect, like width and height, as well as a source and a position. The antialiasing attribute I added because I think that sometimes images do not render that well on mobile devices and you need to help them a little.

These are some of the improvements that I think are good and should be implemented into our project. You can also add a lot more to the application, such as a bit more flair and visual fidelity, but for the purpose of teaching you how to build and make a Qt application I think this is enough. Here you can see our finished results:

2.4.3.9 Adding Local Storage

As I already mentioned, we want to implement a local storage solution in this application. The applications we built so far were all without storing or saving any data to databases or files. This is fine for most applications, but sometimes you want to save data, or have it in multiple locations at ones. And for that purpose, you would want to use a database.

If you want to know more about databases you can check the index to find the section where I talk about them. But for now, let us build ourselves a local storage solution.

First you can go ahead and create a JavaScript file. This can be done the exact same way you would create a qml file. You should give the file Database as its name, and when you are done with that you can create the file.

New JavaScript file

The feature we are trying to use here is called local storage, which is a feature provided by Qt that enables us to create an SQLite Database locally on the device we are running our application on.

I love using this, because you have your own local database and therefore it is extremely fast. And even more importantly, you can create all of your functionality without a remote database, making development a lot easier.

dbInit function

```
function dbInit()
{
    var db = LocalStorage.openDatabaseSync("Database", "", "App Settings",
    1000000)
    try {
        db.transaction(function (tx) {
            tx.executeSql('CREATE TABLE IF NOT EXISTS app_settings
            (data_text, data_value)')
        })
```

```
    } catch (err) {
        console.log("Error creating table in database: " + err)
    };
}
```

The first function we can create in our Database.js is the dbInit function. Because we want to work with a database throughout our application, we need to initialize it somewhere, and this will be done in this function.

First we create a variable called db, then we initialize this db variable with opening a database sync through LocalStorage. The values you see inside the brackets are necessary, so fill them out. The only ones really important are the name in the front and the length at the back. For most applications, the length is not really important as you will probably not create so many thousands of items.

Below the declaration of the db variable we have a try-catch block. This checks to see if the database exists, and if it does not then it creates the database with the correct data fields. If it is not able to create the database or initialize the database connection it will give us an error.

dbGetHandle function

```
function dbGetHandle()
{
    try {
        var db = LocalStorage.openDatabaseSync("Database", "",
                                               "App Settings", 1000000)
    } catch (err) {
        console.log("Error opening database: " + err)
    }
    return db
}
```

The next function we need is our dbGetHandel. This function only exists so that we can save some code in other functions we will create later. In dbGetHandel we only have a try-catch block that tries to open a database connection. This is the same openDatabaseSync function we had earlier, so you can copy it down. The catch again prints out an error when it occurs.

Now we can look at the dbSet function, which creates a new item in our table. The function starts by us giving it two variables, data_text and data_value. Whenever we want to call dbSet we need to give it these two values.

dbSet function

```
function dbSet(data_text, data_value){
    var db = dbGetHandle()
    var rowid = 0;
    db.transaction(function (tx) {
        tx.executeSql('INSERT INTO app_settings VALUES(?, ?)',
                    [data_text, data_value])
    })
}
```

Next we call the dbGetHandel function, which opens up our database connection if the database exists. Then we call db.transaction, which will open a transaction, and in this transaction we can now execute our sql.

The sql we have here is basic. We have a prepared statement that inserts a new item into data_table, our table with the values data_text and data_value. It is a quite simple sql statement but it does its job, and if you know anything about sql you have probably written this a million times already.

The dbGet function is the next in line, and as the name suggests it is used to get an item's value. As before, our function starts with initializing db with our database connection using the dbGetHandle. We also need to give our dbGet function data_text as a property so that we can interact with it later.

dbGet function

```
function dbGet(data_text){
    var db = dbGetHandle()
    var rowid = 0;
    db.transaction(function (tx) {
        var result = tx.executeSql('SELECT data_value FROM app_settings
        WHERE data_text="'+data_text+'"')
        rowid = result.rows.item(0).data_value
    })
    return rowid;
}
```

Next, we create a new variable called rowid, which will alter be used to return out value we selected.

The actual sql we need to run is again fairly simple. It starts by us opening another transaction and then executing our select inside of that transaction. The sql we execute is a simple SELECT that grabs the data_value from data_table where the data_text is equal to what we provide the function with. As you can see here, we do execute the sql in the standard way, but putting it into a variable this is commonly known as a result set. Now this result set holds an object of our data. This is not any good as with just an object there is not that much to do, so we need to get the data_value out of our object. We call our variable rowid and set it to result.rows.item(0).data_value, which will give you the data_value.

To find out what I needed to call to get the data out of the object, I just used the standard local storage example as the code template. I took a lot of the functionality from there, and I would advise you to do this too. The local storage example from Qt is extremely well structured and great to read through, so I recommend giving it a look.

Next, in the function I printed out the result in a console.log; this is not necessary, and I only did this for testing purposes so you could leave it out if you want to. Lastly you need to write *return rowid* after the function. This is a basic SELECT using sql on a table, but it does the job for us so it is completely fine.

dbUpdate

```
function dbUpdate(data_text, data_value)
{
    var db = dbGetHandle()
    db.transaction(function (tx) {
        tx.executeSql(
                    'update app_settings set data_text=?, data_value=?',
                    [data_text, data_value])
    })
}
```

The dbUpdate function is next. The only reason we are going to write this is because I want to show it to you and because it is also a great way to write the functionality we want.

Basically it is the same function as the dbSet, except that we do not use INSERT as our sql statement but UPDATE. This is again a prepared statement as before, and here it works by looking if it can find the data_text we want to update, but if it does not find it will just create it, and if it finds it, it will update it to the new value.

With the dbUpdate function writing we now have all the functions we need for our application, so let us implement them.

New added imports

```
1   import QtQuick 2.15
2   import QtQuick.Controls 2.15
3   import QtQuick.LocalStorage 2.12
4   import "Database.js" as LocalStorage
```

The first thing we need to do is add two new imports into main.qml. The first new import is QtQuick.LocalStorage. This is needed because our JavaScript file requires this for the functions that you get from it. The second import is just our database. To better use our database inside our main.qml, we need to set an alias for it. Here I have gone with database, as that is what we are working with. But you can choose another alias if that suits you.

```
37   Component.onCompleted: {
38   LocalStorage_Settings.dbInit()
39   }
```

The next thing we need to add on main.qml is the dbInit(). We need this to be able to interact with the local database (if you are not sure what I mean by this go back a few pages, where you can find a more thorough explanation).

```
12   property var winCount: LocalStorage.dbGet("playerWin")
13   property var losCount: LocalStorage.dbGet("playerLos")
```

Finally, we need to change the winCount and the losCount. Before they were just integers, which was fine if we did not want to connect to a database, but here we need to call our database with its alias and call the function dbGet() with the correct data_text. When the application now starts up the database will open up and the data for these to property is being loaded.

This is in my opinion the best way to work with databases in Qt, and it works. There are other more elegant solutions, such as wrapping this Database.js file in a component and only having the component interact with the application, and that would be the correct way of doing it when you want to make it professional. But for our purposes this is not necessary, and we achieved our goal of getting data from the local database.

The only problem is that currently there is no data attached to these data_texts. This is because we did not create the data. To do this, we first need to go to our Player_Phase. qml file and change a few lines.

The first thing we need to change is again the imports, which here are the exact same as the ones in our main.qml, so you might just want to copy them over. If you think that this is not necessary to add these imports at this point, because you think we already did this in the main.qml and that has all the other files linked to it, then you are mistaken.

The current structure we have does not allow us to simply have the imports and components in one file and use them from there; for that we would need a better project structure. Nevertheless, we need to add the imports and then we can continue.

```
1    import QtQuick 2.15
2    import QtQuick.Controls 2.15
3    import QtQuick.LocalStorage 2.12
4    import "Database.js" as LocalStorage
```

After that we can also add the Database.dbInit to our Component.onCompleted event. We already used this, but to give you a refresher on what it does, whenever the Item component at the top is being loaded and rendered the function inside of this is being called. It is a wonderful option to call functions right at beginning of the application.

```
112    Component.onCompleted: {
113    LocalStorage_Settings.dbInit()
114    }
```

Lastly, we can add the set and update function to our onClicked event of our application. I used both the updated and set function here. You can only use one or both, but basically here they do the same: they take our win- or losCount and add them to our data_text and then add them to the database.

As you can see, with two lines of code you can add data to our database. This is exactly the power behind the local storage component of Qt: it makes it extremely simple to write a basic database and use it in your application, and you can interact with it extremely easily and change all the things you want.

```
105    console.log(winState)
106    gameFrame.setCurrentIndex(1)
107    //upload to local storage
108    LocalStorage.dbUpdate("playerWin", winCount)
109    LocalStorage.dbSet("playerLos", losCount)
```

With that we are done with writing and creating our local storage solution. If you were to run our application now, you will see that when you start the application, the win- and losCount are null. This will immediately change when you get a loss or a win through the application.

If you were to now close the application and start it back up again, you will see that the data is loaded and the correct value displayed. We are now done creating our local storage.

This is not nearly enough of what you need to learn to work with databases, as you will need a lot more experience and actual practice with working with them. What I provided here was an overly simplistic and broken-down version of how to get started, and now you are able to start learning more about databases, how to interact and manage them, and how to best implement them in your applications.

Next, we are going to deploy our application to a mobile device so that it works on there too.

2.4.3.10 Deploying the Application to Android

We already deployed an application to a mobile device in the last project we did, and this is not going to be very different. We are doing it here because I want to teach you a little bit more about how to do this, and because I want to show you that the local storage also works on mobile. We are not going to go over all the thing we need to do to make the deployment to work; my main focus will be on how you would best set this up if it were a production release we were doing.

If you want a little bit more context and explanation you can go to the end of the last project we did, the Hang-Man project, and have a look at the section where we deployed the application to Android.

Here we start by opening up the project tab at the left of the screen.

You can see the list of different build and run kits Qt offers us. If you only selected MinGW 64-bit as I did, all other kits are currently disabled. The only kits that are important to us you can see at the top of the list. These are the different Android kits you can build for. Why are there so many different kits, you might ask? This is because of the Android Operating-System open-source. That means anyone can use and build their own version of Android, and that is exactly what people have done. You could even do this yourself if you have the time and dedication for it.

Combined with the simple fact that there are different chipsets and producers of Android phones, you are left with a lot of different kits we need to account for.

But we do not need to develop for all kits out there. In development you should only focus on your device you want to run the application on for development. Later on you can focus on others, which will then be not too hard as Android versions are not so different and most applications do not really require any changes or special configuration to run properly.

I select the arm64-v8a as my kit; you should choose the kit that corresponds to your own device. If you do not know what kit you need to use, the best way is to run the application with any of the different kits enabled.

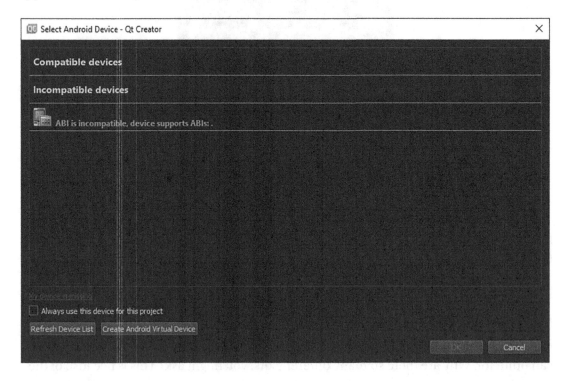

This will open up this wizard, which is used to select the Android device to run our application on. Currently we do not have any device connected to my machine so nothing is shown, so let us connect a device to our machine. This should be done with a USB-Cable, as that is the best way I know of.

If your device is now connected to your machine you can refresh the list with the button on the left.

Your device should now be visible on screen. It might happen that the device is shown as being incompatible, but this probably just means that you need to check a dialog box on your device to allows access to it.

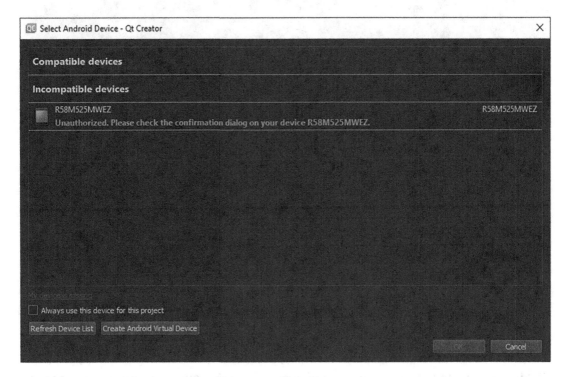

If you do not get this message or the dialog you need to figure out how to get your device into development mode, which is different for all devices, you need to go to the device setting and click the version number several times, and then you can enable developer mode.

If you did all this you can refresh the device list again and the device should now be compatible. If that is still not the case, then you need to start one of the other kits Qt has to offer and see if that one works, but normally Qt will tell you which kit to use next to the device. You only need to run it with that kit enabled. For me, this is arm64-v8a.

You can also see the current Android version as well as other kits that would work with it here. When you have selected the correct kit, you will see the following wizard:

When you see the preceding page, you can click ok. This will start building your application and deploying it to your device when finished.

This can take upward of a few minutes depending on your machine. If everything is working as expected you will see your application popping open on your device and you can now start playing with it. You can also look at the Compile Output, which sometimes can be quite interesting. To look at it, you need to go the bar at the bottom of our Qt Creator window and click on the Compile Output tab.

```
Android package built successfully in 35.052 ms.
 -- It can now be run from the selected device/emulator.
 -- File: D:/qtDev/build-Rock-Paper-Scissors_Game-Android_Qt_6_0_0_Clang_arm64_v8a-Debug/andr
Warning: QML import could not be resolved in any of the import paths: QtQuick.Controls.Windows
Warning: QML import could not be resolved in any of the import paths: QtQuick.Controls.macOS
```

When you see this, you know that the application was built successfully and everything worked as it should. This is also the case when the application launches on your device.

Now you can say that we are done with deploying our application.

But I also want to discuss a few key features in the template you can create for your Android builds. We already created one the last time we built an application for Android, so first let us do that again.

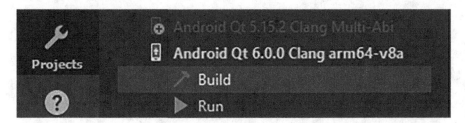

First we need to go back to our Projects tab on the left of Qt Creator, and there you need to open up the build setting for your kit. Next you need to open up the Build Android APK drop-down.

This will be presented to us, and we do not need to sign in to our application this time. Again, click on the Create template button in the middle.

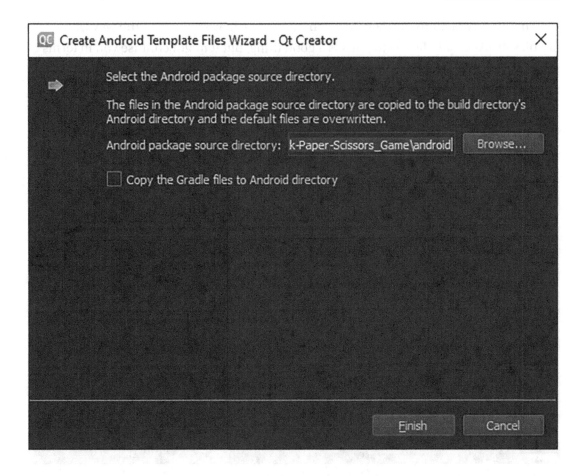

The wizard that opens up can be more or less ignored again, as it does not hold anything we really need at the moment. Click finish and let us continue.

This can take a moment, but Qt will now add the Android Manifest and other necessary files to your project and then open the Android Manifesto for you. If that happens, we can have a look at it. We are not going to fill everything out again, as we already did this last time and it is not really necessary for us here. I just want to talk about two features that are important to me.

The first one is the Style extraction and Screen orientation.

I already talked about them in length the first time we had a look at the Android manifesto, but I want to add a few things and remind you of a few more.

The style extractions and screen orientation are a new addition to the way Qt handles the Android Manifesto. This is a good thing, but it might confuse you in terms of what all the features do and what you can use them for. I recommend not using them for the most part.

First are the style extractions. They are good and they have their uses, but most times you should leave it at the default. Next is the screen orientation, which is something I can see people use quite a lot.

Here you can see a list of all the currently available screen orientations. This can be very overwhelming for a new user, but all it does is tell Android what orientation the screen should be. This means for instance that when you select portrait here, the application will not rotate or turn when you tilt your phone into landscape mode.

This can be extremely helpful depending on the application you want to build, and is in my opinion the best way to get this behavior. It is a really nice addition to the functionality of building Android applications with Qt.

Lastly, we have the splash screen. This is also a new addition to Qt for Android and is an extremely helpful new feature. Before we needed to build complicated loading and Load- and Main-Page setups to build applications we want. And I showed you how to this, because on desktop you will need it so that you can display a loading screen.

But for Android we have this now, and I am really grateful for it. It makes building applications with Android so much easier and faster, and your applications will look far more professional and well realized. Just be sure to use a good high-quality image as the splash screen, and you are good to go.

With that we are more or less done with deploying our application to Android. If you want to learn more about this, go review the Qt Docs on the matter and maybe read the project Hang-Man again to figure out how to do this in a little bit more detail.

2.4.3.11 What We Learned

We certainly learned a lot of different things in this section, and I hope you enjoyed it. I know we only skimmed over some things, but nevertheless I think that we were able to learn something new and important that helps us understand how Qt work and how we can best use it.

Let us review what we have learned with this project:

- **Qt Local Storage**

    This is a local SQLite database that Qt has under its hood. It works like any SQLite database: you can execute your standard array of sql statements and interact with the database from the comfort of JavaScript and Qml. Because it is local it is extremely fast, reliable, and works extremely well with any model or component that you want.

    In my opinion it is the perfect way to build and manage local data and your databases needs, and I have used it extensively over the years. I only gave you a brief interdiction of how this works and how you can interact with it, but I still hope that this can help you learn about databases in Qt.

    Also, as side note, if you want to work with remote databases, you will need to use C++. It is not too hard to set up and works remarkably similar to other languages and frameworks out there (though unfortunately we do not have the time to cover it here).

- **SQL in Qt**

  Here we only briefly touched on the subject of SQL in Qt and I only explained enough so that you understood what we were doing. If you want to learn more about how to work with SQL, the different statements, or other things you can do with it you should read another book or watch a video on the topic.

  What we learned was how to write an INSERT, SELECT, and UPDATE and how to write each in a prepared statement. If you know a bit more about SQL then you understand that these are the most fundamental commands you have in SQL, but for all others this is the perfect starting point with which you can do a whole lot and that should be quite enough for your first few applications.

- **JavaScript functions in external files**

  This is something that seems a little trivial but is especially important if you are building larger applications. Writing JavaScript functions inside of your QML files will not be always possible. It is extremely hard to read and understand if you have a large code base, and it leads to misunderstanding and confusion when you are not careful.

  Here they were perfect to minimize the code we would need to write double or triple, and they showed how you would decrease your code footprint substantially.

  I hope you learned quite a lot in this section and that the lessons and tools I showed you made it possible for you to work now on your own applications that require databases or storing data locally. You can always refer to this chapter if you need an example and if you want to learn more about local storage, and you can always review the local storage example and documentation provided by Qt. They are an extremely good read for anyone who want to know more about Qt and how it works, and they will help you understand the concept better and implement it in your applications.

CHAPTER 3

Components, Features, and Things to Remember

Now that we are finished with three applications we wanted to build, there is not a lot we need to do now. This chapter will review the basic and most used components in Qt, some features you will need to know all the time, and a few things that are essential for building applications.

This includes Databases, JSON Git, and other topics. These were all not essential for us before, but they are heavily used in development in nearly every project. Knowing at least a little bit about them will help you a lot along the way.

The following sections will only scratch the surface of what these subjects and components can do or mean for a developer. The main point is to give you a little bit of information about everything so that you have an easier time starting to learn about them.

3.1 Components

Explanations for the components can be found in the Qt Docs and on the Internet in general. What I will do is first is to explain the component briefly, and then give an example and a few tips and tricks.

This is only a quick rundown of the fundamentals of the component and what belongs to it. Still, this is a really great place to read up on components you want to use or to consult if you have problems setting up the component the way you want it.

© Ben Coepp 2022
B. Coepp, *Introducing Qt 6*, https://doi.org/10.1007/978-1-4842-7490-3_3

3.1.1 List View

List Views are the backbone of any application you wish to make. No matter the size, experience, or scope of the project, you will use List Views. They are essential in providing and displaying data, and there is no real way around them.

The two main things a List Views consists of is a delegate and a model. Both components will be discussed later. The List View itself is the link between them: it takes the data that the model holds and pushes it through the delegate, and out comes an item that displays the data you wanted.

List Views are extremely versatile, and you will always find a use for them. For instance, you will use them creating lists, such as tasks or time tracking. They can be aligned horizontally and vertically, and you can change the direction and the transitions of all the items inside the List View. As you can see there are many things, but what are the main ones?

- **A lot of customization through a lot of attributes**

  If you have a look at the documentation of the Qt List View on Qt Docs, you will find that it has a lot more attributes, signals, and methods then other components. There is a good reason for that. As many people use the List View in all kinds of ways, it is important that there are many options to customize and control how the List View works. This mean that there is less building custom components to supplement a List View, and more a tinkering with the attributes to achieve certain visual components.

  If you have followed along with the projects we did so far, there were many different attributes we used in conjunction with the List View.

- **Interconnectivity**

  Data and visualizing are the main point of a List View. As we will discuss later with the model, Qt provides a variety of data types, and the List View works with all of them easy and fast.

  There are also a lot of custom-built models, like the JSONModel or custom List Views, that provide a totally different way of getting data and displaying it.

- **Fast build time**

   The standard List View is built in a matter of seconds. The basic
   elements you need to build a List View are a width and height, and
   model and delegate. These are all the elements you need. There
   might be a lot more options you have and even more attributes
   you can tinker around with to achieve a perfect List View for your
   type of application, but generally you do not need much to build a
   functional List View.

Overall, the main purpose of the List View is to provide an easy, reliable, and fast
way to build, manage, and most importantly display data. It is one of the most essential
components in QML that you are bound to use all the time. I recommend you trying out
the projects we did, where we are using List Views in a variety of different ways.

Also important is the fact that there are two more views in Qt: the Grid View, and
the Path View. They are fundamentally identical to the List View. The only difference
is that the Grid View is structured like a grid, and there is no difference otherwise. The
Path View is the same thing, as there the elements are displayed on a path. You should
read up on all versions if you have the time for it, as it might be better sometimes to use a
specific version over the others, but because they are functionally the same you will not
need to learn completely new components and how to use them.

Simple List View with Model and Data

```
4    ListView {
5    width: 300; height: 300
6    model: ListModel {
7    ListElement {
8    Name: "Bill Smith"
9    number: "555 3264"
10   }
11   ListElement {
12   name: "John Brown"
13   number: "555 8426"
14   }
15   ListElement {
16   name: "Sam Wise"
17   number: "555 0473"
```

```
18   }
19   }    delegate: Text {
20   text: name + ": " + number
21   }
22   }
```

This is the most basic and standard List View you can think of. For a List View to function you need only a few things: a width and a height or a property, a model, and a delegate.

Closeup of model and delegate

```
7    ListView {
8    width: 300; height: 300
9    model: ListModel {
10   ListElement {
11   Name: "Bill Smith"
12   number: "555 3264"
13   }
14   ListElement {
15   name: "John Brown"
16   number: "555 8426"
17   }
18   ListElement {
19   name: "Sam Wise"
20   number: "555 0473"
21   }
22   }    delegate: Text {
23   text: name + ": " + number
24   }
25   }
```

The model and the delegate property are the most important parts of the List View. Without them there would not really be a List View. They act as the data for the List View and the way the data is going to be displayed.

We are going to talk about how the Model and the Delegate work later on, but in general this is how I would define them. You should probably read up on the section about Qml List View on the Qt Docs, because there are a lot of great examples as well as insights in the documentation.

3.1.2 Stack View

Stack Views are the essential loading, navigation, and displaying pages component in Qt. They function like a door: you have a single component / page displayed at a single given time, and then you can line up all the other components you want to display next, and when you give the command the current displayed item will be changed to the next one.

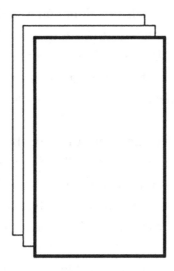

The best representation you will find on the Qt Docs, as you can see here: perfectly shows that you can only have one item currently on display and that behind that are a lot more items that you can switch to when needed.

This is a real performant and reliable way of displaying and retrieving pages or components. It does not take too much space and memory from the user, and even more importantly, it does not require a lot of code to build. The only few things you need are a width and height, and an id by which you can call your Stack View later to change the item displayed, and lastly an initial item that will be the first to display. This simplicity allows for an exceedingly high speed to integrate and test this type of loading pages and providing them for use. Also, when you display a page or component through this Stack View you are able to call onto the functions and ids that are inside said component or page, meaning you can interconnect and bind all your pages and components together.

The most common way I use the Stack View is for the Load and Main Page setup and navigation in my application, and for navigation through a lot of different pages. Both are extremely widespread uses for the Stack View. There are also a lot more interesting uses and unique things you can do with it. The best way to learn about the Stack View is by following the projects and tutorials in this book and trying it out on your own.

We do not really need an example here as we have already built plenty of different Stack Views over the last few projects. But if you want a refresher about them, I suggest you look at the beginnings of the projects where we built the Load and Main Page setup.

3.1.3 Swipe View

Left, Right, Up, and Down these are all directions you would expect to be able to swipe in a mobile application. That is exactly what this component allows you to do. In general, you can say that swiping is one of the best ways to interact on a mobile device.

You can switch views in and out of pages and drag navigations from the top or the bottom. They all allow you to make your entire application more interactable and easy to use.

The Swipe View is one of the components that work best in conjunction with other components. If you want to make a menu that allows your users to switch between different views, then you might want to use a Swipe View. While it does not allow for complete control over the swipe actions, if you investigate what you can find on the Qt Docs you will see a lot of attributes then can allow you to create tight and interactive controls for your applications.

They are one of the most used components in Qt Quick, and if you want to build applications for the mobile device you will probably use a Swipe View. The number of things you can do with it are good, and we even build a few applications on our own with the Swipe View, for that see the Hang Man project.

To give you a simple and precise example, let me show you what a simple Swipe View looks like:

Simple Swipe View

```
4    SwipeView{
5    id: swipeView
6    width: 720
7    height: 640
8
9    Item{
10    id: item1
11    }
12
```

```
13    Item{
14    id: item1
15    }
16
17    Item{
18    id: item1
19    }
20    }
```

This is the most basic Swipe View I can think of. A basic Swipe View consists of a width and height and an id. Next, we have our items inside of our Swipe View. Swipe Views are a quite easy and simple way of adding multiple pages and page navigation to an application. On mobile devices in particular, you want to have the ability to swipe on your device to switch views or pages.

If you want to learn more about Swipe View, I suggest you go to the Qt Docs and read up on them and go to the last few projects and review how we used the Swipe View.

3.1.4 Buttons

What framework would be complete without a way to interact with your UI? The best way and most widely expected way is by using buttons.

Button

There are a lot of ways you can interact with a button in Qt, and I will list some of the ways I use to interact with them here:

- **Clicked**

  This is something that most people probably expect: you can click a button. This will be most likely be the most used way you interact with a button. It is easy to use, quite easy to understand, and it works.

- **Double-clicked**

  This is also easy to grasp: when you click a button you can also double-click it. The nice thing is that this functionality is already prebuilt as a signal in Qt. Otherwise you would need to manually build this, which is possible but not so easy to do.

- **Pressed and Released**

  This is also fairly easy to understand: you can press a button and release it. The main reason you would want to have this is that you can differentiate between the press and the release of a button. So if what you want to build is reliant on precise timing, this is great.

- **Press and hold**

  As with the clicked signal, this is one of the ones you will use so often. It tracks the time you press the button and when this time is longer than a specific fresh hold, a signal is triggered. This is great for a delete button or function.

- **Toggled**

  If you have a checkable button, this signal is emitted when the button is enabled or disabled. This is great for options.

  You can also style buttons in any way you want, from borders, to the background, or you can add icons or anything you want to it. This allows for near limitless possibilities for creating your own styled buttons. There is also another button type that you might want to use, the round button, which is in functionality the exact same as the normal button, but it has rounded corners. You could build your own round button by applying a rounded rectangle as the background component of the round button, but Qt provides you with a simpler and more elegant alternative.

The best way to experience what you can do with a button is by using it, so make yourself a project and try out whatever you want. I have built a small library of custom buttons with all types of styling and functionality. This is also a great thing on your portfolio if you want to make the some yourself.

Here are two examples for some simple buttons that you can build yourself. These are not really fancy or anything special. but they are a good example what buttons can do.

Simple Button with onClicked event

```
9    Button{
10   id: button
11   text: "Simple Button"
12   onclicked: {
13   console.log("You clicked a Button")
14   }
15   }
```

This is the simplest button you can have: you have a text property that represents the text that is going to be displayed on the button. You also have the onClicked event. Without this a button is pretty senseless, so probably you will always have some sort of press, click, or hold event that triggers some functionality. This is all you need for a simple button. It is nothing fancy or special, but you will tend to use this quite a lot.

Simple Button with onClicked event and background element

```
9    Button{
10   id: button
11   text: "Simple Button"
12   background: Rectangle{
13   anchors.fill: parent
14   colors: "red"
15   }
16   onclicked:{
17   console.log("You clicked a Button")
18   }
19   }
```

The background property available for all buttons is also important. In most cases when you want to build something really unique or design-heavy you will tend to run into limitations with the normal buttons. Mainly they are not flexible on their own for these kind of purposes.

But what you can do is use the background property and give your button a complete and custom background. This is really helpful and powerful, and can make it a lot easier to build and design your application.

3.1.5 Mouse Area

The Mouse Area is simply and honestly a button. It has the same functionality as the button and you can even build a button from it, but it also has some functionality that is larger than that of a normal button. So let us have a lock at what you can do with it. The Mouse Area can visually be explained as a rectangle that has all the functionality of a button and more, but this rectangle is transparent.

As with the normal button you have all the standards to click, press, and hold signals, but also some new ones. Mostly they revolve around the hover functionality you have in when you use a mouse. If you want to build anything custom with hover functionality you will most likely use this as your starting point.

Another thing that you can do with this is drag and drop. Mouse Areas have built in drag functionality, so if you want to build anything with drag functions then you can do this right here.

This brings me to the main point about the Mouse Area, which is that it is the perfect starting point for building your custom controls and interactable content. Because it does not have any prebuilt elements inside of it, you can have complete freedom over how and what you want to build.

Here is a quick example for a Mouse Area:

Simple Mouse Area

```
 9    MouseArea{
10    id: mouseArea
11    width: 200
12    height: 200
13    onclicked:{
14    console.log("You clicked a MouseArea")
15    }
16    }
```

As I already said, the best way I would describe a Mouse Area is as a transparent button without any text. You can place everything inside the Mouse Area, such as images or more complicated design elements.

3.1.6 Text Field

Text Fields are one of the most used components in Qt. You will use them throughout development from the tiniest input to the largest application, and they are essential for doing any kind of importing from normal data such as strings or integers dates.

The component text field is not really that difficult to understand. Generally, you can say that the text fields attributes or properties can be divided into two categories, one which is the visual attributes such as with height or font size color, and the other is the more programmatic attributes such as the length of the input methods input masks different eco modes displaying text options.

All these properties in conjunction leave us with a good option of imputing different types of different forms of text. I would even go as far as to say that the text field is the one most useful option and component for in putting any kind of data into your application. The visual properties you can set include hide color and font types; generally you can say that there are no real limits to what you can do with a text field. I recommend that you stick with the more common ways. Of course you can create outlandish news designs or custom text fields that have their own styles and their own way of interacting with the input data, but this is not easy. Also, for the properties concerned with the data itself they all revolve around the fact that you can manipulate the data that is being served from the user into the application. so you have echo mode you have input checking things like this and then you have things that the results around the fact that you can display the text provided by the user in a specific format or in a specific mask.

An example of why is this is important is with password input in your application. You generally do not want to have the password when you type it in displayed in a raw text format that someone could view by looking over the shoulder of your user. That's not really a good option, and for that we have something called the input mask, which takes the inputted streaming and converts it in such a way that only the specific characters we wants to display are shown, or are they are converted to specific characters that reflect the type of text we want to display. For passport for instance this would be the * sign.

Simple TextField with echoMode

```
 9   TextField{
10     id: mouseArea
11     width: 200
12     height: 200
13     placeholderText: "Password"
14     echoMode: TextInput.Password
15   }
```

This is a good example of what I mean with the password functionality. You can use the echoMode to manipulate the display text into something different. In this case every letter would be changed to *. A better solution in my opinion would be done through another echoMode.

```
14   echoMode: TextInput.Password
```

This echoMode displays the newly added letter for a short period of time and then changes it to * after.

There are also other options of inputting data: number inputs, Cara cells, and different text areas, for instance with which you can put more text in with just a text field. They are also really great and work wonderfully for the type of application you want to build, but if you just want to put in some numbers or a little bit of text such as the title or name you will most likely use a text field.

There is also no real going about using anything else if you follow the common tutorials and instructions for using input fields in Qt. If you want to put any kind of data into your application you will come across the text field in a lot of tutorials. There are as already mentioned other ways to put data in your application and then work with the data, but the number of properties and methods and signals you have on command with the text field are outstanding and, in my opinion, so flexible that there is no real problem creating very highly integrated inputs that you can work with and manipulate in such a way that there are no real limits to what you can build.

We already used the text field multiple times in our applications, the best example being the input for our data in our ListView that can be found in our first real project. In my opinion the best way for learning how to use the text field is by first checking out the Qt docs and trying to understand how the ListView works, and then figuring out different ways you can create inputs. I usually do this by just searching online for designs of specific inputs or just using applications. Many applications have wonderful types of inputs with complex design and structural elements, and there is a lot you can learn from just checking the inputs out and trying to implement them on your own.

To make it easier for you to work with text fields, I will give you a small example here:

```
9    TextField{
10    id: mouseArea
11    width: 200
12    height: 40
13    placeholderText: "Placeholder Text"
14    }
```

As you can see, a simple text field consists out of a width and a height. This is the simplest version you can build. I always add a placeholder text property to the text field, as I think that without it the user would most likely not be able to use the input effectively because they do not know what needs to be input there.

The best way to learn about text fields is to build them yourself and try to build some resembling ones that you can find online.

3.1.7 Rectangle

Rectangles can be rendered with a solid color, gradient, or a border.

They are the most useful tools for building your UI, and their versatility is better than anything else. To illustrate my point, I am going to list a few attributes that enable the rectangle to be so versatile.

- **Color**

If you want a color as the background of your application, the rectangle has this option.

- **Gradients**

You can create any gradient you want. This replaces the color attribute, and you can gradient between two or three colors depending on your options.

- **Rotation**

You can turn and rotate the rectangle in any direction you want, enabling you to create a multitude of different shapes and perspectives.

- **Radius**

This is the best option available if you want to round the corners of the rectangle. Unfortunately, you can only round all corners at the same time. If you only want to round specific corners you will need to use an interesting trick: use a primary rectangle where you round all corners, and then use one or two rectangles that are only on the side where you do not want round corners, and then you can overlap the rounded corners with that rectangle. The rectangle should have the same color or gradient as the primary rectangle. And with that, you have a rectangle that visually as only specific corners rounded.

With all these attributes you can create any number of forms and shapes you want. There are no limits to what you can build using this. I wish there were more examples of advanced manipulation of rectangles on the Qt Docs, but unfortunately the only real option you have right now is figuring out the things on your own or using this book as example to build what you want.

Here is a quick and easy example of what a rectangle looks like in code:

Simple Rectangle with color

```
9    Rectangle{
10   id: rec
11   width: 200
12   height: 200
13   color: "red"
14   }
```

As you can see, we only need a few properties: most of the time this is only a width and a height, and a color. You can also use the standard positioning properties to place the rectangle wherever you want. Rectangles are the perfect way to build background element in your project.

3.1.8 Delegates

Delegates are in their simplicity data-aware masks used in conjunction with a View and a Model. The View takes the data from the Model and pushes the data into the Delegate. This enables an extremely fast and easy development process of building and visualizing data.

You can use any form of component you want, and you can also build them data-aware and easer then you might think.

We used them a few times before when we built a ListView, so if you want to refresh your knowledge then you might want to reread that part of the book.

If you want an example of a working Delegate, you should review section 3.1.1, "List View," where is a functional example. There is also a simple example of a Delegate here:

```
21   delegate: Text{
22   text: name + ": " + number
23   }
```

This is a quite simple example of how a Delegate functions. You will always have a component that displays the data from the Model. That is all the Delegate is for. In the preceding example we have a Model that has the data endpoints name and number. These we can then add together as a string and print out.

Normally you will tend to only use the Delegate in conjunction with a Model and a List View.

3.1.9 Models

As with any programming language, at one point or another you will need to work with data. There are a lot of ways to do this: you can use Arrays and Lists, and in Qt you will use Models, which are ArrayLists where you can put in Items that house your data. There are a lot of different ways to do this, and you have different data Models provided by Qt like the List Model, which provides the basic functionality you want from a list data structure. If you are familiar with List Arrays in Java you will quickly get the hang of the List Model.

Some things you need to know about Models in Qt are:

- All data inside the Model is provided as named data roles

- You can easily bind Qt Models to Qt Views

This means that it is quite easy to get the data from the Model into a view, which works by using the named bindings and pulling the data for each item out of them. This is a wonderful feature that allows a quite easy way to create data that can be visualized. This means that no matter what you build and how complicated the model gets, if you have the correct binding you can always pull the data you want.

There are a lot of different Model types out there. Some you might see a lot are:

- **List Model (as already mentioned)**

- **XML Model**

XML is a wonderful definition language that allows the creation of highly integrated and nested data structures. It lends itself well to Qt if you receive your data that way.

- **Object Model**

If you come from an object-oriented programming background you will be familiar with the objects inside lists and this is no different. It greatly enhances the way you can build applications, as you are not limited to only bindings.

- **Integer Model**

I myself have not used this model, but you use the integer as a Model that houses several types.

- **Object Instance Model**

If you only have a single object type, you can use the object instance as a Model.

- **C++ Data Model**

This is the real maker of Qt, giving you full fixability over all the different ways you could model your data. You can use Qt's own model structures and different data types, or you can use the common ones like Arrays Lists and the like.

As you can see there are a lot of ways you can use Models inside your application. There are also many more. I briefly touched on some of the different ways here, but you should also review them if you need them later. The best way to do this is by using the Qt Docs, where you can find examples as well as explanations about all the different Models and how you can best set them up and use them.

In this book we also used a Model, the List Model, for displaying simple data. This the most widely used option Qt provides. If you need to review that knowledge you can also reread parts of this book.

3.1.10 Custom Components

This is one of the things that makes building applications with Qt so easy and great. You can build your own components and reuse them anywhere in your application. To most people this is nothing new, as a lot of other frameworks also provide this as a core concept.

The way that involves these core concepts:

- Having the attributes for the custom component the user can interact with

- All the functionality for the component is handled inside of the component, and no matter where you use the component its functions stay the same

- You can reuse the component in multiple instances and throughout a project

These are the fundamental things you need to know about custom components in Qt. They are remarkably like the ones you would find in a lot of other frameworks, so let us have a look at how to create a custom component.

We are going to create a custom button that when clicked opens another button above it, and when you click that button it disappears and you get a console log. This is simple and not hard to understand, but it lends itself well to learning the topic at hand.

```
RoundButton{
    id: root
    width: 40
    height: 40
    background: Rectangle{
        anchors.fill: parent
        radius: 99
    }
    property var isOpen: false
    onClicked: {
        if(isOpen == false){
            addButton.visible = true
            isOpen = true
        }else{
            addButton.visible = false
            isOpen = alse
        }
    }
}
```

```
RoundButton{
    id: addButton
    visible: false
    width: parent.width
    height: parent.height
    anchors.bottom: parent.top
    anchors.bottomMargin: 10
    onClicked: {
        console.log("Hidden Button was clicked")
        addButton.visible = false
        isOpen = false
    }

}
}
```

Here we have a perfect example of what a custom button should look like. We have our first-round button, with a width, height and id to match, as well as a background component. Most importantly we have a property, which is exposed so that we can use it inside of our button, but also outside if we wanted to.

Inside this button is then our other round button. We interact with both buttons by using the onclicked event, and as you can see, they open and close themselves when you click them. When you click the inner add button we will get a console log.

This right here is the power of a custom button. You can hide a lot of logic that under normal circumstances would be recreated on many different pages a lot of times, and here you can just build it once with all the functionality that is needed and then use it whenever you need to.

3.1.11 Qt Charts

Qt Charts are an amazing tool to visualize and display data in a variety of ways, from simple pie charts and line charts to some really complicated and advanced charts such as candle charts. Qt offers nearly all of the charts your heart can desire, or that are commonly used in data visualization.

This section will be split into three parts. First we will set up Qt Charts, because it does not work right from the get-go. Next, we are going to create one chart from the Qt Docs that is more or less boilerplate code, but I want to show you the different ways a chart can be displayed and how they work, and how they are built. Lastly, we are going to create a custom candle chart that is styled and displays some stock data.

All of this is just the tip of the iceberg, but we do not have the time to create everything on our own, so we are going to skip over some parts. If you want more information, then you might want to review the Qt Docs for more information, where you can find anything from the properties you can use to some boilerplates you might want to try out.

Now let us edit a simple Hello World project in such a way that we can use Qt Charts. First you need to create a simple Qt Quick Hello World Application.

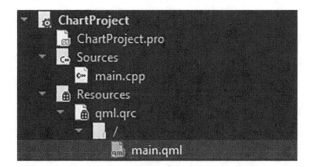

We do not need any new files, or anything special. Next, we can edit our main.qml file. We need to update the imports to the newest version, delete the QtQuick.Window, and add the QtQuick.Controls to our main.qml. We should also change the window to a ApplicationWindow. We have already done this a few times, so you should be familiar with it, but here is a screenshot of what your main.qml should look like:

```
1   import QtQuick 2.15
2   import QtQuick.Controls 2.12
3
4   ApplicationWindow{
5   width: 640
6   height: 480
7   visible: true
8   }
```

Next, we need to import QtCharts. The newest version at the time of writing this is 2.3, but if you have a newer version that please use that.

QtChart import

```
3   import QtCharts 2.3
```

If you have done everything as instructed, then you will get an error that QtCharts is an unknown component. This has two reasons. First, we need to change a few things in the main.cpp and .pro file of our application. The second reason is only important when you are using the Qt 6.0, because in this version QtCharts is not included. If you want to use Qt Charts you would need to drop down to Qt 5.12 or later. But Qt is bound to be updated, and Qt Charts will be included. So please follow the next steps before switching the Qt version.

```
 1  QT += quick
 2
 3  CONFIG += c++11
 4
 5  # You can make your code fail to compile if it uses deprecated APIs.
 6  # In order to do so, uncomment the following line.
 7  #DEFINES += QT_DISABLE_DEPRECATED_BEFORE=0x060000    # disables all the APIs deprecated before Qt 6.0.0
 8
 9  SOURCES += \
10          main.cpp
11
12  RESOURCES += qml.qrc
13
14  # Additional import path used to resolve QML modules in Qt Creator's code model
15  QML_IMPORT_PATH =
16
17  # Additional import path used to resolve QML modules just for Qt Quick Designer
18  QML_DESIGNER_IMPORT_PATH =
19
20  # Default rules for deployment.
21  qnx: target.path = /tmp/$${TARGET}/bin
22  else: unix:!android: target.path = /opt/$${TARGET}/bin
23  !isEmpty(target.path): INSTALLS += target
```

.pro unchanged

This is a comparison of the standard .pro file you will find in your project and how it should look.

It is important that you add in line 1 *gui core widget* behind quick. This will enable Qt to run the qui widget components that are normally unavailable in Qml Quick Applications. I also updated the C++ version to a newer one; this is optional, but I would recommend that you always use a newer version of C++.

.pro changed

```
1   QT += quick gui core widgets
2
3   CONFIG += c++11
4
5   # You can make your code fail to compile if it uses deprecated APIs.
6   # In order to do so, uncomment the following line.
7   #DEFINES += QT_DISABLE_DEPRECATED_BEFORE=0x060000      # disables all
    the APIs deprecated before Qt 6.0.0
8
9   SOURCES += \
10  main.cpp
11
12  RESOURCES += qml.qrc
13
14  # Additional import path used to resolve QML modules in Qt Creator's
    code model
15  QML_IMPORT_PATH =
16
17  # Additional import path used to resolve QML modules just for Qt Quick
    Designer
18  QML_DESIGNER_IMPORT_PATH =
19
20  # Default rules for deployment.
21  qnx: target.path = /tmp/$${TARGET}/bin
22  else: unix:!android: target.path = /opt/$${TARGET}/bin
23  !isEmpty(target.path): INSTALLS += target
```

Now to the main.cpp file, because we need to edit it also. The basic thing we need to change here is the type of QApplciation Qt uses under the hood.

Normally Qt uses the QGuiApplication as the application type to render the basic Qt Quick Applications. This will not do for us; we need the QApplication for our type.

```
1   #include <QGuiApplication>
2   #include <QQmlApplicationEngine>
3
4   int main(int argc, char *argv[])
5   {
6       if (qEnvironmentVariableIsEmpty("QTGLESSTREAM_DISPLAY")) {
7           qputenv("QT_QPA_EGLFS_PHYSICAL_WIDTH", QByteArray("213"));
8           qputenv("QT_QPA_EGLFS_PHYSICAL_HEIGHT", QByteArray("120"));
9
10  #if QT_VERSION < QT_VERSION_CHECK(6, 0, 0)
11          QCoreApplication::setAttribute(Qt::AA_EnableHighDpiScaling);
12  #endif
13      }
14
15      QGuiApplication app(argc, argv);
16
17      QQmlApplicationEngine engine;
18      const QUrl url(QStringLiteral("qrc:/main.qml"));
19      QObject::connect(&engine, &QQmlApplicationEngine::objectCreated,
20                       &app, [url](QObject *obj, const QUrl &objUrl) {
21          if (!obj && url == objUrl)
22              QCoreApplication::exit(-1);
23      }, Qt::QueuedConnection);
24      engine.load(url);
25
26      return app.exec();
27  }
```

Unchanged main,cpp

There are no other changes we need. There is a quite different structure when you compare the two different versions, but they function the same. When you create an application you will probably never notice the difference.

But we need these changes, so change your main.cpp to the version you can see in the next screenshot. Also remember that Qt updates the main.cpp regularly, so it might be the case that there is a newer version with which you can achieve the same result.

Changed main.cpp

```
1   #include <QApplication>
2   #include <QQmlApplicationEngine>
3
4   int main(int argc, char *argv[])
5   {
6   QCoreApplication::setAttribute(Qt::AA_EnableHighDpiScaling);
7
```

```
8    QApplication app(argc, argv);
9
10   QQmlApplicationEngine engine;
11   const QUrl url(QStringLiteral("qrc:/main.qml"));
12   QObject::connect(&engine, &QQmlApplicationEngine::objectCreated,
13   &app, [url](QObject *obj, const QUrl &objUrl) {
14   if (!obj && url == objUrl)
i.   QApplication::exit(-1);
15   }, Qt::QueuedConnection);
16   engine.load(url);
17
18   return app.exec();
19   }
```

When you have changed the main.cpp and the .pro file, you can go and rebuild the project. This can be done by right-clicking on the Qt project and then selecting rebuild. When you have done that you can see that the error about QtCharts not being found as a module has vanished, and we can finally start building our first chart.

Simple Pie Chart

```
5    ApplicationWindow{
6    width: 640
7    height: 480
8    visible: true
9
10   ChartView{
11   anchors.fill: parent
12   antialiasing: true
13
14   PieSeries {
15   id: pieSeries
16   PieSlice { label: "eaten"; value: 94.9 }
17   PieSlice { label: "not yet eaten"; value: 5.1 }
18   }
19   }
20   }
```

This is the simplest and easiest way to understand how a chart works in Qt. With the basic Pie Chart, its data needs to always consist of two things: the value and the label.

All charts need to be located in a Chart View, which is a container for the actual chart. It has a height and a width, and you can also set a few more properties such as anchors, antialiasing, theming, and animations. The Chart View can be best compared to something like a Scroll View.

Inside a Chart View you will find some sort of Chart Series. These are always named after the type of chart they represent, like Pie Series in this instance. These Series only there to tell the Chart View what type of chart it is and how the data should be displayed.

Lastly there the actual data elements, which here are named Pie Slices as they represent the slice of the pie. Each Series has their own different type of data. They fundamentally work the same, consisting of a value, label, and a color, and possibly a few other attributes.

As you already know from the List View or List Model, you can add, delete, and modify existing Pie Slice or any data of a Chart Series. This allows you to make interactive charts, and you can also be assured that you have complete control over the elements.

Now we can create our own candle chart, which we are going to fill with our own data. This will not be too difficult.

Simple Candlestick Chart

```
9    ChartView {
10   title: "Candlestick Series"
11   width: 400
12   height: 300
13
14   CandlestickSeries {
15   name: "Acme Ltd."
16   increasingColor: "green"
17   decreasingColor: "red"
18
19   CandlestickSet { timestamp: 1435708800000; open: 690; high: 694;
     low: 599; close: 660 }
20   CandlestickSet { timestamp: 1435795200000; open: 669; high: 669;
     low: 669; close: 669 }
21   CandlestickSet { timestamp: 1436140800000; open: 485; high: 623;
     low: 485; close: 600 }
```

```
22   CandlestickSet { timestamp: 1436227200000; open: 589; high: 615;
     low: 377; close: 569 }
23   CandlestickSet { timestamp: 1436313600000; open: 464; high: 464;
     low: 254; close: 254 }
24   }
25   }
```

As you can see, it is remarkably similar to the other charts. It consists of a Chart View, a Candlestick Series, and Candlestick Sets. The only difference is that the data is a little bit different than before. We do not only have one value, but four different values. You have the open, close, high, and low values, and all of them combined in this chart leave you with a candle stick that represent the data we have put in. Now we want to style this chart, as it currently does not look that exciting.

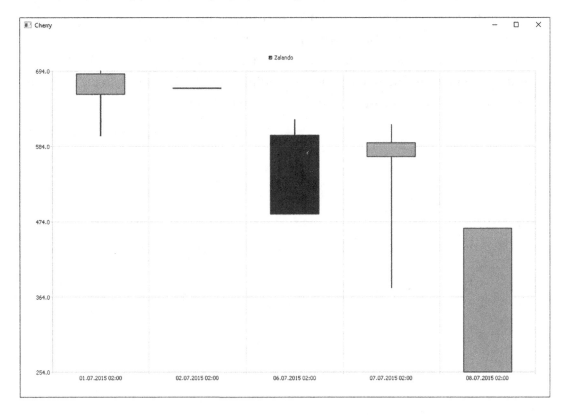

Styling charts is not really difficult. First, you have the option of changing the increasing color and the decreasing color, as you can see in this screenshot. I choose the colors green and red for that, as they are commonly used and clearly readable.

The second option of styling charts is by using the themes property.

Constant	Description
ChartView.ChartThemeLight	The light theme, which is the default theme.
ChartView.ChartThemeBlueCerulean	The cerulean blue theme.
ChartView.ChartThemeDark	The dark theme.
ChartView.ChartThemeBrownSand	The sand brown theme.
ChartView.ChartThemeBlueNcs	The natural color system (NCS) blue theme.
ChartView.ChartThemeHighContrast	The high contrast theme.
ChartView.ChartThemeBlueIcy	The icy blue theme.
ChartView.ChartThemeQt	The Qt theme.

Different Chart Themes

Here you can see some of the different chart themes that Qt provides. It is possible to do custom styling for every aspect the chart has to offer, but it is not really necessary.

I chose the Chart Theme Dark, as it is particularly good in my opinion. I would recommend you look at other themes and find what you like, and when nothing fits what you want you can create them or maybe try building your own theme, or create a custom styled Chart. Here is a screenshot of what this theme looks like:

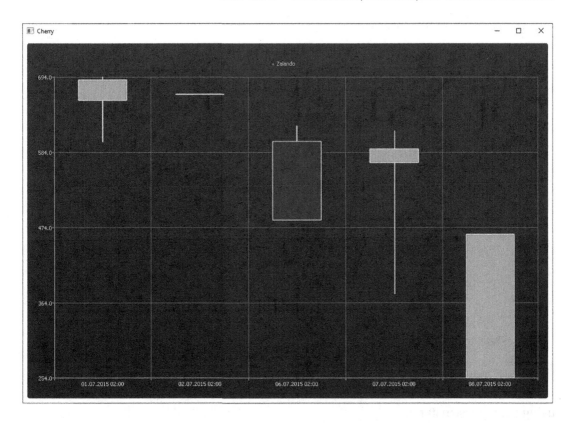

Now that you have an overview of what Qt Charts has to offer, the best way of learning how to use it and what would best fit your own project is to try building your own and displaying some data in it. Qt Charts are extremely versatile and easy to use, and they provide you with a very great way of displaying data in a variety of ways.

3.1.12 JSON for Beginners (and How You Might Use It in Qt)

If you want to build any form of application, you need to work with data. This data can be in a variety of forms, such as the already discussed models or databases. But there is also another way using JSON as your data model.

```
{
  "firstName": "John",
  "lastName": "Smith",
  "isAlive": true,
  "age": 27,
  "address": {
    "streetAddress": "21 2nd Street",
    "city": "New York",
    "state": "NY",
    "postalCode": "10021-3100"
  },
  "phoneNumbers": [
    {
      "type": "home",
      "number": "212 555-1234"
    },
    {
      "type": "office",
      "number": "646 555-4567"
    }
  ],
  "children": [],
  "spouse": null
}
```

Here is an example of what JSON looks like. JSON allows you to group data together using data types, instance:

- **Strings**

- **Integers**

- **Arrays**

- **Dates**

- **Boolean**

You can also use more complex data types such as Arrays. JSON is very versatile, and you can create any form of data structure you want. It is perfect for lightweight data structures that enable you to quickly store and retrieve data.

There are two ways of using JSON in your application. First, you can use the QJSONModel, which are C++ functions that you can use to convert a JSON Model to a C++ Model with which you can then interact normally as with any other model or class.

The other way is by using an Open-Source component, the JSONListModel. This can be found at `https://wiki.qt.io/JSONListModel`. You can import the files you need from the link on the wiki, and then you have access to a QML component that is nearly identical to the one that the List Model QML comes with.

These two methods provide you with a perfect way of building applications and interacting with JSON as your data. You can work with it in Qt and when you need to, or you can create your own JSON data.

If you want more examples of JSON go visit the Qt Docs, where you can find a few examples of how to work with the C++ Models and the QML Components.

3.2 Features

Here are some of the features I want to talk about outside of the context of the tutorials. The first is the C++ Integration. Depending on how deep you want to go into learning Qt and how ambitious and large the application you want to build is, it will be essential to use C++ as your backend. Next are the Translation Files, a lesser known features Qt provides that is used in a lot of Qt applications, but not a lot of tutorials shine a light on how to best use it.

3.2.1 C++ Integration

C++ Integration is a specific and difficult topic that is hard to understand in the context of Qt. There are a lot of resources and tutorials about how to set up C integration, and I will not showcase the flexibility and the power behind using C++ as our application backend here. My goal is to show you how to set up the integration and fire up some small functions. The real power behind C++ integration comes from knowing how to work with C++ and using the power of C++ for building applications. If you know C++ you can immediately start developing complex interactive and highly performant functionality in your application.

But those who do not know that much about C++ and how to work with it, you will be learning how to set it up and if the need arises, how to use C++ in your application. At times there are specific functionalities that do not work with the native components and functionality provided. It might be true that most of the components you will ever need are already implemented in QML, but if you want to work with files like JSON files, for instance, you will need to do this using the C++ functions provided by Qt, and these can only be accessed through the C++ back end.

How can we best set this connection up? First, we need to create a new C++ Class in our Qt Quick application. We are going to do this from a basic Qt Quick Empty template:

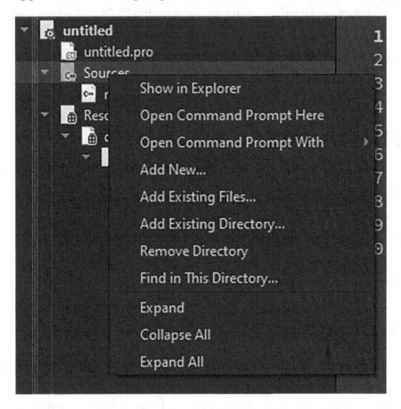

The best way to create the needed C++ Class is by creating it in our Sources. So right-click on our sources and select Add New.

This will open up a similar wizard to the one we commonly used for creating our QML files. Here we need to go under C/C++ and select C++ Class. This may also be automatically selected, but if not then go to it and click choose.

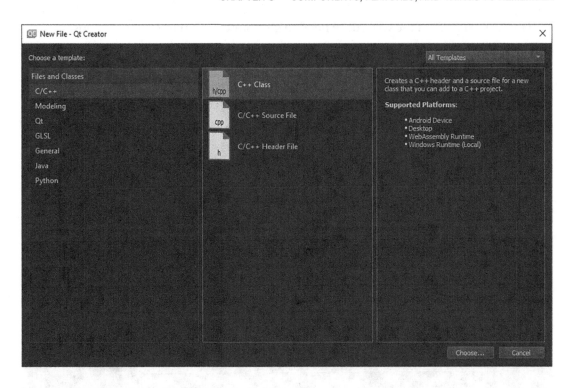

On the next page of the wizard we need to give our class a name. Here I choose MyCustomComponent, as we are creating our own C++ component that we then can use.

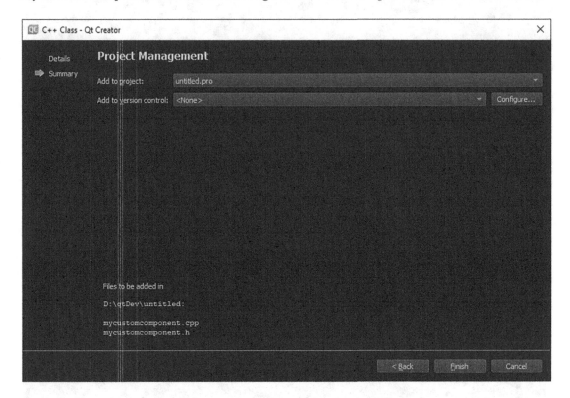

We could add it to our VCS, but we do not need that right here so click create.

If you have done everything as instructed, two new files should be created. The first is the .cpp file of our custom component, which will be below our main.cpp, and the other one is the header file for our custom component.

```
1    #define MYCUSTOMCOMPONENT_H
2
3    #include <QObject>
4
5    class MyCustomComponent : public QObject
6    {
7    Q_OBJECT
8    public:
9    explicit  MyCustomComponent(QObject *parent = 0);
10
11   Q_INVOKABLE void doSomething(QString input);
12   singals:
13
14   public slots:
15
16   };
```

You should fill the header of our component with the preceding code. I will not go into too much detail on what we created here, but just know that line 11 represents the method we are going to write next that will be invokable in QML later.

```
1    #include "mycustomcomponent.h"
2    #include <QDebug>
3    using namespace std;
4    MyCustomComponent::MyCustomComponent(QObject *parent) :
     QObject(parent)
5    {
6    }
7    Void MyCustomComponent::doSomething(QString input)
8    {
9    qDebug() << input;
10   }
```

The code for our mycustomcomponent.cpp looks like this. In lines 8 to 11 you can see the method we created: a simple function that takes a string input and writes it to the console.

This is quite a simple function, but it works and it is a good representation of how the component can also take inputs and work with them.

```
17   QQmlApplicationEngine engine;
18   qmlRegisterType<MyCustomComponent>("MyCustomComponent", 1, 0,
     "MyCustomComponent");
19   const QUrl url(QStringLiteral("qrc:/main.qml"));
```

Line 18 needs to be added to our main.cpp. Currently our component is finished, but you could not do anything with it. For that we need to register the component as a type. This makes it possible to use it in QML.

When you added this line to your main.cpp you can then import our component into the main.qml file we have.

```
1   import QtQuick 2.15
2   import QtQuick.Window 2.15
3   import MyCustomComponent 1.0
```

Next you can add the component into the content for our main.qml and give it an id. As we want to access the functions behind the component, we can use the Component. onCompleted to execute the function when the application finishes building.

Lastly, we only need to call the function and give some sort of text with the function so that it can be displayed.

```
11   MyCustomComponent{
12   id: myCustomComponent
13   }
14
15   Component.onCompleted:{
16   MyCustomComponent.doSomething("Hello fromC++")
17   }
```

If you have done everything up to now, you should get a console output with the string you put in:

```
14:41:48: Starting D:\qtDev\build-untitled-Desktop_Qt_6_0_0_MinGW_64_bit-Debug
"Hello from C++"
QML debugging is enabled. Only use this in a safe environment.
14:41:50: D:\qtDev\build-untitled-Desktop_Qt_6_0_0_MinGW_64_bit-Debug\debug\un
```

As you can see, this is a really good way to build up functions and tools for which you need more functionality than the common QML components. It is not hard to set up or use, and once you get the hang of it you will probably tend to use it from time to time, as it can be simpler to do things in C++ instead of hustling around with difficult QML models and custom components.

My recommendation is that you try to use C++ from time to time in your projects, because you can build extremely great functionality through this. You also have complete control over all the C++ models and classes Qt has for you, so no matter what you want to build you are able to do so.

3.2.2 Translation Files

Something I see all the time in forums is the question, "Does anyone actually use the translation files?" And the answer is yes, there are a lot of uses for them, and there are a lot of people using them.

In tutorials online or in books you will not often find them, because for development you do not need them; development is usually only done in one language. Normally you would not think about adding other languages until the very end of development. All tutorial series, books, or videos generally tend to focus on the first few steps in learning about a language or framework, and even the better ones tend to skip over some parts.

But using translation files is not as hard as you might think. Using them heavily relies on the fact that all the text attributes you want to be changed by your translation file need to be in the correct format, and need to have qstr before them. This is the best way to use the translation file. After that you need to link the corresponding word with the translated version.

Generally, I can say that the best use for a translation files is at the end of your development when the actual publishing and deploying of your application takes place. Remember that this exists and learn about it later if you really need it.

3.2.3 Git in Qt

Git is one of the technologies that you will find everywhere in development. It is the basic tool most developers use to work together on projects.

Git is a free and open source distributed version control system designed to handle everything from small to very large projects with speed and efficiency.

Git is easy to learn and has a tiny footprint with lightning fast performance. It outclasses SCM tools like Subversion, CVS, Perforce, and ClearCase with features like cheap local branching, convenient staging areas, and multiple workflows.

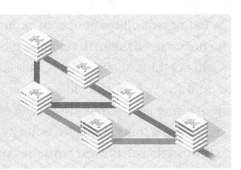

What is Git, from https://git-scm.com/

What Git is should not be that difficult for most people to understand. But how can it be used in Qt, how easy is it to set up, and should you use Git?

When you create a new Qt project you are asked if you want to use a VCS, which stands for Version Control System. There are a lot of different Version Control Systems out there, and one of them is Git. When you set the project up with this option enabled, Qt will create a .gitignore file. This file simply tells Git that some files cannot and should not be added to the repository.

Qt Creator also made the project a Git Repository, meaning that you could immediately push it to a remote repository or share it with the world. This is pretty much the same as you would do with any other project or application you might have.

Now is Git the best option for Qt? That depends on what you typically use. When you are familiar with Git then you will find that this is the same as with any other Git project. Different Version Control Systems tend to work like Git, such as AWS with their Code Commit.

I recommend that you always use some sort of Version Control. This may seem like a basic thing to say, and I know that most people probably already use some sort of Version Control already. But when you have anything larger than a calculator, I advise you to use Git or another Version Control System. It is so much easier to build and develop applications when you use a VSC, and especially with Git; everyone uses it, which is good to keep in mind when you are searching for a new job.

Recruiters tend to look for these skills, as they are essential for companies. You will always develop with other people and because sending files between developers is not that performant or user-friendly, VSCs are the perfect solution.

We used Git only in one project in this book, the Rock-Paper-Scissors Game. There we set up a new repository and uploaded our project to Git Hub. It was a good example of how you probably need to do it when you need to use Git in the project.

3.2.4 Qt Animation

Animations are a big subject when you want to create applications for mobile and desktop devices, and nowadays nearly every framework has some sort of animation framework. Qt is no different in that regard. Animations have been available for a few years now and are currently at a particularly good point when it comes to available features.

What types of animations das Qt have, and how are they different from each other?

- **Property Animation**

As you should know by now, components in Qt have properties attached to them such as width, height, and anchors. These can be manipulated through Property Animations.

Example from the Qt Docs

```
1    PropertyAnimation {id: animateColor; target: flashingblob; properties:
     "color"; to: "green"; duration: 100}

2
```

```
3    NumberAnimation {
4    id: animateOpacity
5    target: flashingblob
6    properties: "opacity"
7    from: 0.99
8    to: 1.0
9    loops: Animation.Infinite
10   easing {type: Easing.OutBack; overshoot: 500}
11   }
```

At the top of this screenshot you can see a rather easy Property Animation. This perfectly represents how an animation is structured in most instances. You always need an id, a target to which the animation is applied, the property you want to change, to what the property should change, and the duration of the animation.

These are the fundamental properties you need for an animation to play. How you then activate and play the animation is up to you.

- **Number Animation**

This is similar to the property animation, and you can see an example in the first screenshot. You can manipulate the numbers behind the properties, such as width, height, x, y, and as in the example, opacity. You could also do this through the Property Animation.

In general, you can say that the Number Animation is a specialized type of animation that best works with number properties.

- **Transitions**

When you want to switch between two pages of a Swipe View, or add or delete an item from a List View, the state of the component is changed. You could do this now instantly so that the change takes place the second you changed the component, or you could apply a transition to the state change.

What a transition does is to link to different states of a component together, and when the state changes the transitions starts playing. A transition is fundamentally an animation, so if you are familiar with the property and number animation you are able to build your own animation.

```
states: [
    State {
        name: "PRESSED"
        PropertyChanges { target: button; color: "lightblue"}
    },
    State {
        name: "RELEASED"
        PropertyChanges { target: button; color: "lightsteelblue"}
    }
]

transitions: [
    Transition {
        from: "PRESSED"
        to: "RELEASED"
        ColorAnimation { target: button; duration: 100}
    },
    Transition {
        from: "RELEASED"
        to: "PRESSED"
        ColorAnimation { target: button; duration: 100}
    }
]
```

Example from the Qt Docs

Here is a fairly simple example of what a transition could look like. You have the different states of your component and then you apply the transition to the state, and when the state is triggered it goes from one state that is declared to another.

Be sure that you have the correct state for the from and to in your transition, because when you have more than two states, it could break the UI really easy when the wrong transition is triggered.

- **Parallel and Sequential Animations**

Now that you know the basic types of animation, how they work, and how to set them up, consider a case where you want to run two or more animations in parallel or sequentially. You could trigger them differently or at the same time, but this is not really that great or performant. For that purpose the Parallel and Sequential Animation exist.

305

```
1   SequentialAnimation {
2   running: true
3   NumberAnimation { target: rect; property: "x"; to: 50; duration: 1000 }
4   NumberAnimation { target: rect; property: "y"; to: 50; duration: 1000 }
5   }
```

As you can see here, both Sequential Animations and Parallel Animations both group animations together, may they be Number or Property Animations.

This enables you to launch multiple animations at the same time, or one after the other. This also allows you to save on code or complicated animation structures.

Now you have a general overview over the different types of animation in Qt, how to use them, what an animation is made out of, and how to set them up. We also covered the Parallel and Sequential Animation, and what they can be used for.

The best way to learn about animations in Qt and how to best use them is to try them out. They fundamentally work the same, and even more importantly the normal animation principals also work on the animations in Qt. You can learn from UX and general animation principals to set up complicated and highly usable animations that enhance the user experience.

3.2.5 Databases in Qt

When you want to create an application that uses data often, and this data needs to be present and saved all the time, most developers tend to use something like a database.

A database is a group of tables you can interact with through the database. You can add, delete, and change table cells and columns. The best way to explain this is with Excel.

For us, the only really important part is that most developers and projects tend to use databases for their high flexibility, and the fact that they are so widely used means that you will find tutorials anywhere you look.

Qt has two ways through which you can use databases. The first is quite easy to explain, as with a lot of other programming languages you have a class that can handle database connections, the results that come from this, and so on. It is an option that most developers are already familiar with through other languages. This is also the option that I would recommend to you. It is widely supported through the Qt C++ backend and it is fairly easy to understand once you get the hang of it. But remember, these functionalities are only assessable through C++. You can create your own component that you can then interact with through QML, but the logic needs to be written and executed in C++. If you are not familiar with C++, then this can be somewhat complicated, but with a little tinkering you will get the hang of it.

The second option is the local storage functionality Qt Quick provides. This is an SQLite Database that you can interact with through QML and JavaScript. It has the same functionality as a normal database, with the exception that it is local.

Here are screenshots of how we set up the Local Storage system in our Rock-Paper-Scissor project. These are the basic functions you will need to best set up your local database:

```
function dbInit()
{
    var db = LocalStorage.openDatabaseSync("Database", "", "App Settings",
    1000000)
    try {
        db.transaction(function (tx) {
            tx.executeSql('CREATE TABLE IF NOT EXISTS app_settings
            (data_text, data_value)')
        })
    } catch (err) {
        console.log("Error creating table in database: " + err)
    };
}
```

First is the dbInit function. This will open or create the database when you call the function. It is essential for using databases in your project, and you cannot go without it.

```
function dbGetHandle()
{
    try {
        var db = LocalStorage.openDatabaseSync("Database", "",
                                                "App Settings", 1000000)
    } catch (err) {
        console.log("Error opening database: " + err)
    }
    return db
}
```

Next is the dbGetHandel function. We do not want to open up our databases every time we call a set or get function, so most of the time you will tend to write a function whose sole purpose is to handle the database connection for our other functions.

If you want a better explanation you can read Chapter 2, section 2.4.3.9, "Adding Local Storage."

```
function dbSet(data_text, data_value){
    var db = dbGetHandle()
    var rowid = 0;
    db.transaction(function (tx) {
        tx.executeSql('INSERT INTO app_settings VALUES(?, ?)',
                        [data_text, data_value])
    })
}
```

The next two functions are the real core of every local storage and database setup. You will always need to get and set data from your database, which is exactly what both of these functions do. The preceding function shows you how to set data in your database. The basic way to do this is just by using a SQL INSERT and then giving the statement the values you want to set.

```
function dbGet(data_text){
    var db = dbGetHandle()
    var rowid = 0;
    db.transaction(function (tx) {
        var result = tx.executeSql('SELECT data_value FROM app_settings
        WHERE data_text="'+data_text+'"')
        rowid = result.rows.item(0).data_value
    })
    return rowid;
}
```

The get function works similarly, but we run a SQL SELECT on our database and then we return the value of the item we get.

These are the basic functions needed for a Local Storage system. You can also connect to remote databases, but for that you will need C++.

I recommend you try figuring out how to best work with databases, what projects need them, and how to set them up. After that you need to learn how to use them, which can be best done through learning about databases in general. All the knowledge you can learn can also be translated into Qt with databases.

3.3 Things to Remember

Here are a few things you should remember. First, Qt is an excessively large and complicated topic with a lot of high-level and overly complicated subjects that are not covered in this book. I will try to provide resources later where you can start learning more about Qt its features and the things you need to know, but be aware that the road ahead after reading this book will consist of trying out things.

Qt is a little bit odd in one sense, and that is the case of where to you it. Some things it can do well, like making Server Applications, Console Applications, and highly integrated and reliant on speed Applications. In these cases, Qt is unbeatable. It simply outperforms anything else, but you get this with one significant drawback: that is the amount of time, manpower, and lines of code you need to get those things done.

A good example is building a Task Manager. You would never do this in Qt. It is a good example with which to learn Qt, and with Qt Quick and QML it can be done quickly and easy but nowhere near as easy and fast as with other frameworks, especially Web-Frameworks. They simply outperform Qt and its building process with sheer ease of building.

Qt has its downsides, but the moment you want to build anything that requires speed, performance, or sheer amount of data throughput, C++ and Qt are the right choice.

In terms of building the application, failure is inevitable and despite the preparation you put into it or the amount of determination and willpower, you will fail and abandon projects. This is nothing bad, and it happens all the time. Even the best of us will abandon a project at some point, and even good developers tend to overestimate the amount they can do. So take small steps, do not overestimate yourself, and especially do not think bad of yourself because you abandoned a project. If the project does not bring you any money and you are doing it for fun, then even those you abandoned are part of the learning process. There is always something you can learn and something new to be had.

And with that I leave you on your own. Do not hesitate to learn new things, and start experimenting with Qt and the features and components it provides. There are so many great things you can build with it, and the only thing holding you back is your own imagination and effort.

3.3.1 Writing Diagrams for Qt

At a certain level and size of a project, you will need to create diagrams. This can be done several different ways, and you can use whatever tool or method you want. But there are a few things that you should always keep in mind while creating diagrams.

Think about the project structure: when you have large and complicated projects that have a lot of QML files and visual complexity, you should always follow that as a guideline with a diagram. This makes it easier to follow along throughout the development process.

The other thing to keep in mind is the naming of files and prefixes. I tend to not follow the naming scheme I have in the diagram in the actual application, which results in a lot of unnecessary problems. If you keep the naming scheme correct you will always be able to find the correct components and refer to the diagram while you create your application.

Lastly, I would recommend keeping a color scheme for the components and the functionality. This makes it quite easy to find the functionality of the component just based on the color of the diagram elements.

Diagrams are in general a good thing to have while you develop, but there are not needed for everything. If you are just designing and programming a calculator, I would not write a diagram. But when you want to build something larger, more complex, and maybe work with multiple people on a project, it might be immensely helpful to have a diagram.

There are a lot of programs out there to write and design diagrams, and they work as you would suspect. But there are not needed to write diagrams; I usually write mine by hand. This is the fastest and simplest way of creating them.

Overall, in general diagrams for Qt are not really that different for diagrams you would use in any other programming project. The tips I provided here are more of the kind that can help you if you have a similar workflow and development process as I have, but you can also find your own preferred way.

3.4 Advanced Topics in Qt

Now we come to some topics that are not as necessary as others, but they still should be mentioned and talked about because they are going to tell you a little bit more about specific topics.

3.4.1 Mobile Applications

We are in the day and age where mobile applications are always in demand and everybody wants to build their own mobile application, and Qt comes with this option. The main features were already implemented quite a long time ago; for instance, the entire Qt quick line-up of components to build things was immediate from the get-go and built with mobile devices in mind, and this is a good thing because in the web development spectrum, mobile devices are always first priority.

Many people only use mobile devices nowadays for consuming media and using applications, and for a business or company that provides any kind of service or product having in mobile application is not only important but sometimes even essential.

As a side note, building Android applications requires a few more steps then just downloading Qt and jumping right in, so please be advised to follow the instructions in the beginning of the book. Sometimes improper setup of Qt can lead to problems and difficulties down the line.

We already covered how to set up Android Studio and how to implement it is in Qt, so here I will just give you some general advice on the way when you want to build mobile applications using Qt.

As we have already discussed, Qt has its difficulties. The best way of solving them is the way you would also do it on a desktop, but mobile development comes with its own share of problems. You will need to learn a lot about how to best make applications for mobile devices, what the best design practices are, and what you actually need to focus on. These things don't really translate from a desktop environment to a mobile device environment, and you will need to learn some things you may take for granted when developing desktop applications. The work you need to do to make a mobile application usable and good-looking with Qt requires little bit of rethinking of how to do things, and you will run into problems that are little bit uncommon and need some time to adjust.

Fortunately, we already built a mobile application using Qt in this book. The Hang Man project was created completely from the ground up with mobile devices in mind, and therefore we could immediately alleviate a lot of problems that would come from developing an application that was not designed from the get-go to be run on a mobile device.

Keep in mind that Qt has been refined and polished over the years regarding developing mobile applications. When I started out developing using Qt I always ran into difficult box problems and I was sometimes the first person on stack overflow to ask questions about specific problems or specific bugs and errors showing up in my code. This was really difficult and sometimes even brought me nearly to the point of switching frameworks, but I prevailed and nowadays this is not really a problem anymore. Most features you will find on iOS or Android are completely usable inside of Qt, and they are much more tightly integrated so that only a specific few features not usable from the start.

If you want to build mobile applications using Qt you will have a lot of options and functionality that were completely alien and unusable in Qt only a few years ago. For instance, Splash-Screens in the Android manifesto with all the different configurations you can do with it Java integration the possibility of using different types of local and push notifications really complicated signals and sensory data that you can use or get from the device is own sensors.

If you are interested in building Android or iOS applications then you are now able to do this: they are not very much dissimilar to desktop applications you could build, and we also discussed how to build them, how to set them up, and how to deploy them. The only thing really left is building something, so get to building it.

3.4.2 Interactive and Real-Time Data

This is a topic a lot of people come up with often while developing applications, as we require connection to a database on hand for large amounts of data. The main way of working with interactive forms or databases in Qt is by making the fields and inputs aware of the data they need to represent. This is best done by using C++ model or anything where you can specify what type of data you actually want to use and what is going from the inputs to your database. You can also use JSON for some things, because there are some external JSON tools and components that you can use that really enable you to make interactive and aware forms and list use that don't require a lot of work to set up.

A good read would be on the Qt Docs found here: `https://doc.qt.io/qt-5/sql-forms.html`.

Generally, this is a topic that is extremely difficult to get a hang of, and you will need to take your time with it. You also need to keep in mind at the start of the development what data you have, so that you are able to test your inputs. Without that you will run in the problem of the inputs not working because you have the wrong data for the job.

Something that users also want to have is a representation to see if what they are doing is correct. This reassures the user that what they are doing is correct, and even more importantly it minimizes the risk of having wrong data inputted into the application. You can also search online for this kind of topic, as there are a lot of great tutorials and papers on the matter. The best I have found over the years are about web development, but the principles are still the same and we can use them for what we are doing. They also provide you with a lot of options on what databases you can use that already have this functionality from the get-go.

What I would use is something like a normal SQL database such as Microsoft SQL Server or SQL Lite. These are perfect options if you have existing databases that have already existing data in them. There is also the option of using something like Firebase or AWS to simplify the process. Both provide you with functionality that can help you create data-aware forms that check what the inputs should be before you need to create your own masks and checks yourself.

In my opinion both options are completely fine, and you can use whatever you want; you should choose what you need and what you know and then go from there.

APPENDIX A

Sources

- **Qt Docs**

  For many of the components, some examples, and representations I used Qt Docs. I did not take any screenshots or text from there, but if you want to be extra thorough then I recommend that you look at Qt Docs for more information on all the topics Qt has.

- **Google**

  You will need to use Google for searching the web and finding what you need. You could use another Service like DuckDuckGo or Ecosia, but I prefer Google.

- **Wikipedia**

  For some of the descriptions of specific concepts I used Wikipedia for reference. While it is not considered a source for academic writing, Wikipedia is extremely helpful for checking basic information.

These are the only outside resources used for this book; everything else is me going through each step very slowly and writing everything out in minute detail. Using my own knowledge and experience makes the book a lot more personal and understandable, and I have the feeling that you can relate to what I am doing.

If you believe I have forgotten a source and you think I should add it, then please contact me via email.

© Ben Coepp 2022
B. Coepp, *Introducing Qt 6*, https://doi.org/10.1007/978-1-4842-7490-3

Final Thoughts

I have tried my best to make this book as enjoyable to read and as fun as possible, and I hope you learned a lot about how Qt works: how to best set it up, work with the components, build applications, and get a general feel about how to work in Qt. I have also tried to be as up-to-date as possible, but I will also provide free updates for eBook readers, and for those buying the book in the paperback version, there should be updates to that version as well.

If you found this to be an interesting, worthwhile read and you want to support me, then I encourage you to leave a review on Amazon to tell other people about this book. If you find any errors or bugs, then go to my website and send me a message or send an email to bencoepp@gmail.com with the subject line "Bug Report a Guide to Qt 6." I will update the book with everything that you think is missing, problematic, or incorrect. Please do not hesitate and give me your honest opinion, as the best way to improve my work is by simply reading your feedback and taking it to heart.

What I would like to leave you with here is to recommend that you start building applications immediately, if you have the time for it. Then start building more and more complex things, figure out what you want to build, make real projects, and try to finish these projects, as that is the best way to learn and understand Qt. You can learn quite a lot from tutorials and books like this one, but in my opinion the best learning practice is by using the framework. At this point you should have a good grip over what Qt has an offer and what you can do with it. This might not be enough to make you a full-blown developer, but experience comes with time. I did not have this experience right out of the box when learning Qt either; this comes with a lot of practice.

There are some good applications to practice your knowledge about this framework, such as xxx, xxx, and xxx, which will help you get to know more advanced topics we could not cover in this book.

With this I leave you, as you have learned quite a lot about this framework, and making things is the important part so go out there do your own thing. Learn about another framework, learn about this framework, learn to develop your projects and brighten your horizon, and I hope to see you with my next book.

© Ben Coepp 2022
B. Coepp, *Introducing Qt 6*, https://doi.org/10.1007/978-1-4842-7490-3

Contact Information

As a reminder, I am providing my contact information here so that you can refer to them when you need to and reach out.

E-Mail: bencoepp@gmail.com

Please include a clear header with your email so that I can easily locate it. I suspect to receive a few hundred emails a day when this book is released, and I will try my best to answer all of them or at least so many as I can manage.

Website: https://bencoepp.io/

If you have more general questions, such as finding links to the things that I used in this book, you can access my website. There you can find out more about me, who I am, and what I do. There is also another contact form where you can contact me, as well as an article and a link to the Amazon page for the book.

Git-Hub: https://github.com/BenCoepp

I use Git-Hub for many things, including the Task-Master and the Hang-Man projects used in this book. Git-Hub is useful for maintaining a large portfolio of good applications as well as for giving you the option of downloading them and having them open while reading. These are quite useful when you are stuck.

Amazon:

If you purchased this book through Amazon or an associated marketplace, you can always ask questions there and I will try to give you a good answer. I also appreciate reviews and any feedback you have to leave, as this will assist other potential readers in determining whether they should by this book instead of any others out there.

Index

A, B

Amazon, 317, 318
Android Studio
  device
    configuration, 36
  devices tab, 35
  download/installation
    download button, 22
    empty folder, 24, 25
    Google Search, 21
    homepage, 21
    installer, 23
    license agreement, 22
    opening page, 23, 24
    progress bar, 26, 27
    quick and
      straightforward, 28
    wizard start menu/shortcuts, 26
  emulator hypervisor
    driver, 32
  features, 35
  license agreements, 33
  pop-up, 32
  progress bar, 34
  SDK configuration, 30–32
  top bar, 34
  USB connection, 32
  welcome page, 29
Animations, 101, 136, 190, 211, 236,
    290, 303–306

C

C++ integration, 295
  connection, 296
  custom component, 298, 299
  home wizard, 296, 298
  main.cpp, 300
  models/custom components, 301
  mycustomcomponent.cpp, 299
  quick empty template, 296
  resources/tutorials, 295
CMake, 31, 45, 46
Components, 267
  attributes, 268
  buttons, 273–276
  core concepts, 282–284
  delegates, 280, 281
  echoMode, 278
  fast build time, 269
  interconnectivity, 268
  JSON, 293–295
  list views, 268–270
  models, 281, 282
  mouse area, 276, 277
  onClicked event, 275
  Qt charts, 284–293
  rectangles, 279, 280
  stack views, 271, 272
  swipe view, 272, 273
  text fields, 277–279
Configuration section, Qt, 28–36

© Ben Coepp 2022
B. Coepp, *Introducing Qt 6*, https://doi.org/10.1007/978-1-4842-7490-3

I

J, K, L

Printed in the United States
by Baker & Taylor Publisher Services